The Relationship Between Chaotic Events and Credit Union Leadership Practices

The Relationship Between Chaotic Events and Credit Union Leadership Practices

Solutions to Chaotic Events in Organizational Cultures

Dr. Paul Withey

authorHOUSE®

AuthorHouse™
1663 Liberty Drive
Bloomington, IN 47403
www.authorhouse.com
Phone: 1 (800) 839-8640

Published by AuthorHouse 05/30/2015

ISBN: 978-1-5049-1307-2 (sc)
ISBN: 978-1-5049-1306-5 (e)

Library of Congress Control Number: 2015908043

About the Author

Dr. Paul Withey currently resides in Houston, Texas. He has over 18 years of credit union experience and has worked with several other industries with management consulting and organizational strategic planning. Valuable transformations continue to occur because of his focus on the bottom up instead of the top down approach. Clients report a significant increase in understanding how chaotic internal and external events can provide organizational opportunities and improve decision making. Dr. Withey uses two models that encourage a new approach to managing organizational chaos. The Organizational Operation Model and Degrees of Freedom Model provide leaders with developing strategies that transform organizational cultures, identify and understand chaotic events, increase effective responses to chaos, and create new operational norms based on chaotic experiences.

Dr. Withey enjoys a work-life balance by pursuing a passion for national and international travel to experience diverse cultures. He is involved with his community, enjoys good food, challenging conversations amongst friends, and heartfelt humor.

Introduction

The purpose of the exploratory qualitative phenomenological research was to explore the experiences of leaders in charge of individual credit unions during a period of economic contraction. Although the research study focuses on credit unions, the research study can be applied to a variety of other industries. Twelve credit union leaders from Texas were interviewed. The general and primary research question of the research study was, "How did the top leaders of certain individual credit unions experience the credit crisis and recession of 2008-2010?" The design selected for data analysis was derived and adapted from the Moustakas method of analysis and phenomenological data. Six significant themes emerged from the analysis of the interviews. These themes were fast pace of change, leadership disagreement on internal and external data analysis, anger, shock, frustration, the need to reduce rumors and fear, external environment seemed chaotic, and the crisis forced creativity. The findings of the research study may strengthen the use of transformational leadership practices among credit union leaders and other business leaders within different industries. Based on the results of this study, it was recommended that credit union leaders, and other business leaders, adopt the organizational operation model and the degrees of freedom model to help leaders increase his or her capacity to manage change when experiencing what appears to be the onset of chaotic events.

Table of Contents

List of Tables

List of Figures

Chapter 1
INTRODUCTION

The credit crisis of 2008 and the ensuing business recession caused many financial institutions of all types to experience operational turmoil (Foo, 2008). The turmoil placed increased and unusual demands on leadership decision making and management practices within organizations making up the financial sector of the national economy, including credit unions. Torn between protecting the balance sheet of the organization and funding customer and community expectations and needs, credit union leaders struggled with a growing disconnect between organizational survival and organizational mission (Thibault, 2007). Asset devaluation, tightened credit, bank failures, and an economy in recession represent the turbulent financial environment that credit union leaders found themselves facing since the crisis began (Blalock, Gertler, & Levine, 2008).

Economic crises, recessions, and depressions are reoccurring events in the economic history of modern nations. Such crises have been regular characteristics of capitalist economic systems at least since the collapse of the Dutch tulip market in 1637 (Schiller, 2005). The cyclical nature of capitalist economic activity has been described, studied, and analyzed in detail by scholars ever since Charles Mackay published his account of the Dutch tulip mania in 1841 (Schiller, 2005). Leaders and managers of banking and business organizations always seem surprised when an economic crisis occurs and the expanding economy in which they operate begins a period of rapid contraction. The intent of this empirical phenomenological qualitative study was to explore the lived experience of credit union leaders as they respond to the first signs of a credit crisis and to the chaotic events of a general business recession.

The results of the research study may add to the understanding of the leadership skills needed to improve responses to decision-making cyclical periods of organizational crisis. When confronted with such periodic crises, leaders should be able to recognize unexpected possibilities, create opportunities, and take advantage of the unplanned outcomes (Pryor & Bright, 2006).

The first chapter includes the background of the problem, the statement of the problem, and the purpose of the study. The chapter also includes the significance of the problem, the nature of the research study, the theoretical framework, and operational definitions of terms central to the research study. The chapter concludes with an analysis of assumptions that may be critical to the argument of the research study as well as the scope, delimitations, and anticipated limitations.

Background of the Problem

Some economists consider the financial crisis of 2008 to be one of the worst economic disasters in more than 75 years (Altman, 2009). Nearly every domestic and global economic indicator had decreased. Many theorists agree that the cause of the economic crisis was rapid expansion of subprime mortgage lending and the sale of speculative subprime investment instruments (Gorton, 2008). The increase in subprime mortgage lending and the sale of subprime investment instruments contributed to a breakdown in the American credit and mortgage system that, in turn, led to the recession (Haro & Sullivan, 2009).

Subprime mortgages are mortgages that possess higher interest rates, when compared to standard prime mortgages, balloon payments, pre-payment penalties, and excessive fees. Subprime mortgages gained in popularity in 1994 due to the introduction of new credit scoring techniques (Johnson & Neave, 2008). These new credit scoring techniques, and decreasing mortgage interest rate pricing indexes, helped to increase the value of subprime lending to $625 billion in 2005, from $35 billion in 1994 (Quercia, Stegman, & Davis, 2007). Individuals with a subprime mortgage were sensitive to changes in economic conditions and were likely to default on their loans when pressure on personal income increased (Quercia, Stegman, & Davis, 2007). To increase financial profitability, financial institutions and investment firms packaged subprime loans with traditional mortgage loans and created asset-backed securities, which sold these securities on the open market (Bordo, 2007). Many investors worldwide purchased these securities and were unaware of the true potential risks of these investments (Bordo, 2007).

Credit unions are member-owned nonprofit financial organizations, with the primary purpose of providing financial services, deposits, loans, and other financial products and services to individuals who share a common bond and are of average financial means (Glass & McKillop, 2006). Credit unions perform in a competitive banking environment and share characteristics with co-operative forms of economic organizations (Glass & McKillop, 2006). These characteristics have fostered credit union expansion in America since the passing of the Federal Credit Union Act (Federal Credit Union Act, 1934), deregulation of depository institutions (Depository Institutions Deregulation and Monetary Control Act, 1980), and passage of the Credit Union Membership Access Act (H. Res. 1151, 1998). These changes in federal laws have allowed credit unions to expand their products, services, and membership flexibility. In 2010, more than 7,554 federally insured credit unions serve nearly 90 million members, with deposits totaling more than $752 billion (National Credit Union Administration, 2010a).

As credit unions have grown in size and complexity, their vulnerability to external environmental changes has also increased. Government regulations and general economic conditions are the major sources of organizational and operational change for credit unions (Barron & Hannan, 1994). During the recent period of credit union growth, credit union leadership considered to increase employee motivation, leaders simply needed to implement, or increase the use of, monetary incentive programs (Siemsen, Roth, & Balasubramanian, 2008). Any such simple behavioral assumption has the potential to impede credit union leadership behavior and decision-making during periods of unexpected change (Basu, Raj, & Tchalian, 2008).

Statement of the Problem

The general problem, establishing the need for the research study, is that the financial crisis of 2008 and ensuing recession created turmoil within the entire financial industry. The turmoil included pressure on deposit insurance funds, monetary market operations, financial institution solvency concerns, liquidity and credit anxiety, and blurred regulatory boundaries (Goodhart, 2008). The turmoil within the financial industry caused financial institutions of different types to experience organizational stress, resulting in poor risk management, increased internal conflict, lost opportunities, and defensive management instead of producing creative leadership (Shiller, 2008). Economic contraction forced leaders to develop strategies that focus on survival rather than on performance (Shore, 2009). In response to the recession, credit union leaders tightened budgets, experienced decreased revenue, decreased employee compensation, deferred branch expansion, and closed branch offices, which caused interpersonal and interdepartmental organizational chaos (Gustafson, 2009). The specific problem investigated is the lived experience of credit union leaders, CEOs, and CFOs, during the onset of the 2008 credit crisis and the contracting economy, from 2008 through 2010. This qualitative research study focused on credit union leadership in the United States, using a phenomenological design. Qualitative research procedures, using interviews with open-ended questions, was appropriate to explore and understand better how credit union leaders respond to organizational crises caused by negative changes in the general economic environment within which they operate.

Purpose of the Study

The purpose of the exploratory qualitative phenomenological research was to explore the experiences, perceptions, attitudes, and behaviors of leaders in charge of individual credit unions during a period of economic contraction. The qualitative method selected is appropriate for the research study because a qualitative method is exploratory and seeks thematic rather than numerical data (Creswell, 2005). The main characteristic of the phenomenological procedure was the use of loosely structured interviews, after which the interview transcripts and observations were reduced to natural meanings, in an attempt to capture lived-world experiences. Phenomenological analysis of the interview transcripts created themes and patters of interest from interview data (Whitty, 2010). An empirical phenomenological design is appropriate because the exploratory research question driving the research has to do with patterns of experience, perception, and behavior, not quantifiable at this exploratory stage of the research.

The phenomenological procedure used requires a researcher to employ an interview technique to collect data on the lived experiences of participants'. The phenomenological collection technique involves collecting original data in the form of naïve descriptions, using open-ended questions, and dialogue with participants (Moustakas, 1994). The data analysis involves the systematic interpretation of the experiences of the participants by asking open-ended questions, reflective analysis from participants', and interpretation of participant responses (Moustakas, 1994). The specific population for the research study was restricted to CEOs, CFOs, vice presidents, and senior managers who influence strategy development in individual credit unions operating within the State of Texas. Each qualifying participant had 10 or more years of experience within the credit union industry.

Significance of the Study

The research may lead to a better understanding of how credit union leaders respond to organizational crises caused by negative changes in the general economic environment within which they operate. The decisions made by leaders can influence various internal organizational variables and the decision-making process can have far-reaching organizational sustainability implications (McKenzie, Woolf, van Winkelen, & Morgan, 2009). In the research, lived experiences of recognizing the signals of impending crisis, on how leaders interpreted crisis signals, and on the relationships between such events and leadership responses to these events were the main areas of concentration.

Credit unions are an important economic alternative to a traditional banking system (Bauer, 2006). As a non-profit cooperative, credit unions exist to serve members with a common bond to promote savings and provide lower cost loan products. Unlike traditional banks, credit unions elect a volunteer board of directors from the membership and each member has one vote. The volunteer board of directors and non-profit structure allow credit unions to provide services to "people of small means" (White & Kleiner, 2001, p. 127) and provide a social purpose of helping individuals achieve their financial dreams, instead of focusing on profits.

The research study may make an original contribution to leadership studies by continuing the effort to apply the perspectives of general systems and chaos theory to an understanding of leadership behavior in times of crisis. This study may also offer a potentially new perspective on a leader's capacity to change his or her approach, based on the needs of the organization, when experiencing what appear to be chaotic events. Such adaptability may prove to be the most effective leadership skill a leader can display (Higgs & Rowland, 2005). The findings of the research study may allow credit union leaders to create new models, recognizing external changes that influence the sustainability of the organization.

Introducing chaos theory into organizational leadership has become a new approach to leadership psychology and philosophy, promising to influence leadership and management theories (Bums, 2002). Chaos theory can help leaders understand disruptions that challenge normal events (Arciszewski, Sauer, & Schum, 2003). The significance of chaos theory for leadership studies lies in its heuristic power. If the challenges to normal events are observed through the lens of chaos theory, organizational leaders may make better-informed decisions in times of uncertainty.

Nature of the Study

The objective of the research study was to report on an exploratory investigation of the lived experiences of selected top leaders and managers of credit unions faced with the crisis of a rapidly contracting economy. When a lack of research in a specific field dictates the need for an exploratory study, qualitative research methods are used (Mason & Staude, 2009). The data required for the planned investigation was the participants' recollections of certain events, perceptions, interpretations, and decisions that occurred during the credit crisis and recession of 2008-2010. Intensive open-ended interviews allowed for obtaining the recollection from leaders of certain events, perceptions, interpretations, and decisions that occurred during the credit crisis and recession of 2008-2010. Because the required data were qualitative, the appropriate research procedure was qualitative. Strength of qualitative research procedures, using interviews with open-ended questions, is that it allows a participant to discuss his or her responses and explore themes with the interviewer during the interview itself (Creswell, 2005; Moustakas, 1994). Since intensive and open-ended interviewing can encourage interaction between researcher and subject, qualitative research may allow for immediate exploration of emerging themes (Breakwell, 2004).

Qualitative research involves interviewing participants to identify themes in the form of words. The words collected, the data, transpire into two categories. These categories include interview data as resources and interview data as topics. A researcher can use interview data as resources to reflect the participants' reality and interview data topics to reflect the participants' interactions with the researcher (Seale, Gobo, Gubrium, & Silverman, 2007). A quantitative research design would not have been appropriate for the research study as quantitative research focuses on a quantifiable phenomenon, on specific variables, and on an analysis of quantifiable categories determined in advance (Schutt, 2009). Quantitative researchers, who attempt to isolate cause and effect, lack the ability to capture individual subjective perspectives because a goal of the quantitative research is to extract and measure experience instead of studying the experience directly (Denzin & Lincoln, 2008). A qualitative research design assists researchers with the study of experience.

The method selected for data analysis, as derived and adapted from the procedures developed by Moustakas (1994), was phenomenological. Interviews were conducted as interactive processes to collect data from targeted participants using a series of data collection procedures (Willis, 2008), including collecting the original data through naïve descriptions, using open-ended questions, and engaging in active dialogue with the participants as they described their experiences. Enriched data from the transcripts of the interviews allowed for reflective analysis and interpretation of the responses to open-ended questions and dialogue (Moustakas, 1994). The goal of this qualitative research was to discover and conceptualize the experience of chaotic events and obtain, as deeply as possible, an understanding of lived experience that describes how leaders within the credit union industry lead and manage organizational performance when experiencing internal challenges prompted by contraction of the external economic environmental.

Research Questions

The use of qualitative phenomenological research approach allowed for the examination of the perceptions top leaders of certain credit unions in the state of Texas regarding the credit crisis and recession of 2008-2010. Findings from the research study may add new knowledge about leadership performance during organizational crises. The general and primary research question for research study was: *How did the top leaders of certain individual credit unions experience the credit crisis and recession of 2008-2010?* Secondary questions helped understand how top leaders of credit union leaders experienced, perceived, interpreted, and reacted to the credit crisis and recession of 2008-2010. Secondary research questions assist in understanding the lived experiences of the research participants. The secondary research questions included:

1. When and how did you first notice the external environmental changes that threatened your organization? What were the danger signals?
2. As the external danger signals increased, what were the first signals of internal dysfunction?
3. How would you describe your perceptions of and feelings about the external and internal situations you found yourself confronted with?
4. How would you describe your emotional and cognitive responses to the external and internal events you were required to deal with?
5. If you have not already done so, would you use the word chaos to describe any aspect of your experiences over the past two years?
6. Using hindsight, were your responses as timely and/or as creative as needed?

Theoretical Framework

Developed by Hames (2007), the theoretical framework for this qualitative research study is the ratchet effect model. For this research study, the ratchet effect model was a heuristic construct to discover whether credit union leaders experience economic recession and organizational crisis as chaotic events. The use of the ratchet effect model was an attempt to map how credit union leaders reacted to internal chaos resulting from external changes in the economic environment. Using the ratchet effect model helped to explain how leadership practices reposition the organization through strategic intelligence, organizational intelligence, organizational capability, and innovative performance (Hames, 2007).

Successful leadership is important to the success of any organization. Successful leadership practices are dynamic, and include three concepts: self, followers, and the organization (Crossan, Vera, & Nanjad, 2008). Organizational capability, operational intelligence, innovation and performance, and strategic intelligence support these three concepts. Each of these supporting concepts interacts with change drivers, which include markets, management, and organization. How leaders experience these change drivers is dependent on an organizational atmosphere that is not rigid, one that allows the organization to experience reform, and develop new values (Carr-Chellman et al., 2008).

Leaders can strengthen the theoretical framework of the ratchet effect model with single loop and double loop learning theory. Leaders may use single loop learning when the internal organizational environment remains relatively stable and current organizational strategies remain sufficient to meet internal and external demands (Bums, 2002). Double loop learning occurs in complex operating environments in which stakeholders can adapt and learn to maximize performance and increase adaptability (Bums, 2002). Leaders that employ single loop learning environments may lack organizational capacity and operational performance, whereas double loop learning environments may increase organizational intelligence, innovation, and performance.

Some management philosophers encourage leaders to recognize the importance of remaining responsive to the demands of external environments through the application of chaos theory (Bums, 2002). Recent organizational research has included topics such as the influence of chaotic events on leadership practices, internal chaos and organizational change, strategic considerations for surviving in chaotic modern markets, and understanding and managing chaos in organizations (Geraldi, 2009; Hughes, 2009; Karp & Helgo, 2009). The controversies in the field include conflicting definitions of organizational stability, arguments over whether external environmental change is the sole representation of disorder, and arguments about the meaning of chaos versus complexity (Peat, 2008; Plowman et al., 2007; Zexian, 2007).

Through chaos theory, an understanding of the relationship between chaotic events and leadership practices is emerging as a new leadership application within the business environment. Recent literature on chaos theory may help leaders manage internal responses to external environmental changes. Chaos theory, as a leadership paradigm, may prove to be useful because of its sensitivity to early and distant conditions in the environment (Arciszewski, Sauer, & Schum, 2003).

Definitions of Terms

The terms, repeatedly used throughout the research, needing definition or further clarification include:

Chaotic events. Chaotic events are temporary changes occurring in complex systems that create uncertainty (Kim, Payne, & Tan, 2006; Yolles, 2007).

Complex dynamical systems. Complex dynamical systems are systems that display characteristics of orderly and chaotic activities with behavior that is unpredictable (Cooke-Davies, Cicmil, Crawford, & Richardson, 2007).

Nonlinear behavior. Nonlinear behavior is often unexpected, unpredictable, random behavior, despite leaders performing in a stable environment (Mendenhall, Macomber, & Cutright, 2000).

Non-periodic systems. Chaotic performing systems influence or attract other systems, called strange attractors, and result in behavior that is unpredictable for both systems (Dolan & Garcia, 2002; Helbing, 2008).

Strange attractor. A strange attractor is a system that never settles at a fixed point and is always moving (Bums, 2002).

Zone of stability. The zone of stability is a zone in which organizations become isolated from the demands of a changing external operating environment (Bums, 2002).

Zone of randomness. The zone of randomness is a zone in which internal and external environments reflect complete anarchy and increase the likelihood of collapsing (Bums, 2002).

Assumptions

In the qualitative phenomenological study, assumptions help direct data collection and analysis (Creswell & Plano-Clark, 2007). I used interviews to investigate the lived experiences of selected top leaders of credit unions faced with the crisis of a rapidly contracting economy. In this research study, several assumptions were made. I had the following methodological assumptions as a basis for the conclusions of the present study: (a) participants were able to recall germane details of their subjective experiences accurately, (b) participants were willing to share their subjective experiences honestly, openly, and completely, and (c) the participants represented the general population of credit union leaders and top managers. Although I used a non-random approach when selecting the participants, I assumed an inherent diversity of participants. My final assumptions were that quantitative phenomenological research assists me capitulated rich and relevant results from top leaders of credit unions through open-ended questions and that my personal opinion or experience did not distort the interview data.

Scope and Limitations

Within the scope of the current study, a qualitative research method helped explore the lived experiences of selected top leaders of credit unions faced with the crisis of a rapidly contracting economy. The scope of the research study was restricted to interviews of CEOs, CFOs, vice presidents, and senior managers of credit unions who influenced strategy development for their organizations. The research was restricted to credit unions within the State of Texas and to participants who have had 10 or more years of experience within the credit union industry.

The limitations intrinsic to the research study were both a function of the restrictions of scope and the limitations of qualitative phenomenology (Bloomberg & Volpe, 2008). The most important limitations were a consequence of the nature of the interview process and participant responses. The use of the phenomenological qualitative research always carries the risk of an unwillingness to share subjective information that is confidential as well as confidential organizational strategies or insights (Creswell, 2005; Moustakas, 1994). As with all phenomenological investigations, success is dependent upon both the quality of the recollections and the honesty of participants during the interview process (Creswell, 2005; Moustakas, 1994).

Delimitations

Delimitations are the boundaries used to establish the outer limits of a research project (Lunenburg & Irby, 2008). The participants for the research study were restricted to credit union CEOs, CFOs, vice presidents, and senior managers who influenced strategy development. Excluded were middle managers and supervisors, because middle managers and supervisors are not usually involved with strategy development. The purposive sample further restricted participants to leaders and senior managers from credit unions located in Texas.

Summary

The credit crisis of 2008 and the ensuing business recession have caused many financial institutions of all types to experience operational turmoil (Foo, 2008). Torn between protecting the balance sheet of the organization and funding customer and community needs, credit union leaders are struggling with a growing disconnect between organizational survival and organizational purpose (Thibault, 2007). The general topic of the research study was to investigate the lived experience of the leaders of American credit unions during a period of economic challenge associated with the credit crisis and recession of 2008-2010. Chapter 1 opened with a discussion of the background of the financial crisis and a brief explication of the specific research problem. A brief statement of the purpose of the research study, a discussion of the academic and social significance of the research study, the research procedures, the theoretical perspective used to interpret the findings of the research, definitions of terms, assumptions made and acknowledged, and the determinations of scope and limits followed. Chapter 2 provides a review of the current literature on the history of credit unions, credit union leadership practices and the current financial crisis. Identification of gaps in the literature covering credit union leadership and a review of recent attempts to use certain concepts and models derived from chaos and systems theory in the explanation of leadership behavior in organizations under extreme stress follow.

Chapter 2
LITERATURE REVIEW

The general topic of the research study is the relationship between the credit crisis and recession of 2008-2010, which created turmoil within the national economy and the concomitant turmoil within the sector of the financial industry composed of credit unions. This turmoil caused credit union leaders to shrink budgets, experience decreased revenue, declining morale, and suspend branch expansion, close branch offices, and caused interpersonal and interdepartmental chaos (Gustafson, 2009). The purpose of this qualitative phenomenological research was to explore the lived experiences of a purposive sample of credit union leaders and managers during the 2008-2010 period of financial crisis. The research study builds on a review of historical, theoretical, and research literature that provide the context for an investigation of credit union leaders when faced with an organization-threatening recession.

Chapter 2 opens with a description of the literature search itself, with a detailed account of the search methods and sources, the titles, articles, research documents, and journals found and evaluated. An historical overview of relevant literature covering the founding, growth and development of credit unions follows. The status of the credit union sector and credit union leadership practices was examined and identification of gaps in the research literature. Because general systems and chaos theory provide the theoretical perspective for the research study, the chapter includes a discussion of the relevant theoretical literature.

Title Searches, Articles, Research Documents, and Journals

The review of the literature presented in chapter 2 includes an electronic search for relevant peer-reviewed books, journal articles, and research documents found in such online databases as EBSCOhost, OneFile, ProQuest, Emerald, InfoTrac, Google Scholar, Google Books, Questia online library, and other internet websites. All journal articles cited were peer-reviewed. Table 1 represents the types and quality of the literature reviewed that were dated pre-2005 and post-2005. The literature reviewed, which includes material related to credit unions, leadership theories, financial crisis, chaos theory, and systems theory, was selected for relevance to the research topic. When appropriate, gaps in the research literature are identified and discussed.

Table 1 Summary of Sources in the Literature Review

Reference Type	Total	Published before 2005	Published 2005 and after
Peer-reviewed journal articles	91	8	83
Books and educational literature	17	8	9
Web sites	10	2	8
Other research	2	0	2
Totals	120	18 (15%)	102 (85%)

Historical Overview and Current Findings

Themes discussed in the historical overview and current findings include the history of credit unions, credit union leadership practices, financial crisis of 2008, chaos theory, and systems theory. The discussion include brief summaries of major leadership theories, specifically path-goal theory, transactional leadership theory, transformational leadership theory, leader-member exchange theory, situational leadership theory, and servant leadership theory, in order to provide context for the research study on credit union leadership practices.

History of credit unions. Originally founded in England during the 1840s, the credit union movement began with a group of weavers seeking an alternative to the traditional banking system (Credit Union National Association, 2009b; Ryder & Chambers, 2009). During the 1850s, credit union cooperatives formed in Germany to serve urban artisans, small shopkeepers, and agriculturists (Guinnane, 2001). The credit union movement began in response to a banking culture that focused on affluent patrons (Guinnane, 2001). Individuals of lesser means often experienced higher costs for credit, with some interest rates totaling more than 30% (Guinnane, 2001).

In 1900, the credit union movement came to North America, with Alphonse Desjardins establishing the first credit union in Levis, Quebec, under the same circumstances found in England and Germany more than 50 years earlier (Credit Union National Association, 2009a; National Credit Union Administration, 2010b). In 1909, Desjardins helped start the first credit union in the United States, located in Manchester, New Hampshire, and in the same year, Pierre Jay and Edward Filene successfully helped create the first credit union act in Massachusetts (National Credit Union Administration, 2009a; Texas Credit Union League, 2008). The credit union movement in the United States was, and still is today, defined as a nonprofit financial cooperative institution owned by its members and democratically controlled to provide members with a safe place to save and borrow at reasonable rates (National Credit Union Administration, 2009a; Nikolopoulos & Handrinos, 2008). The primary purpose of a credit union is to accept deposits and provide loans to member-owners (Ryder, 2008). A volunteer board, elected from the membership, governs credit union operations and upholds the credit union philosophy of "not for profit, not for charity, but for service" (National Credit Union Administration, n.d., para. 15). From its American founding in 1909, within just three decades, the credit union movement in the United States had grown to include more than 3,300 credit unions serving more than 641,000 members in 39 states (Credit Union National Association, 2009c).

By 1960, more than 6 million people belonged to more than 10,000 federal credit unions (National Credit Union Administration, 2008a). In 1970, the National Credit Union Association and the National Credit Union Share Insurance Fund were formed to insure member deposits (National Credit Union Administration, n.d.; Sharma, Ghosh, & Sharma, 2007). In 2008, more than 8,600 federally insured credit unions served more than 85 million members with deposits totaling more than $600 billion (National Credit Union Administration, 2008b). As of December 2009, more than 7,554 federally insured credit unions served nearly 90 million members with deposits totaling more than $752 billion (National Credit Union Administration, 2010a).

Current credit union leadership practices. Leadership development in credit unions has focused on innovation, management characteristics, organizational performance, and organizational design (Pleshko, 2007). As credit unions have grown in size and complexity, their vulnerabilities to external environmental changes have also increased, specifically with changes in government laws and economic conditions, which increase the need for individual and organizational accountability, self-analysis, commitment to growth, and adaptive learning (Marques, 2007). Credit union leaders can exhibit a particular leadership behavioral bias, which is the belief that to increase employee motivation during periods of difficulty, leaders need to implement, or increase the use of a monetary incentive program (Siemsen, Roth, & Balasubramanian, 2008). Behavioral bias has the potential to influence credit union leadership behavior and decision-making (Basu, Raj, & Tchalian, 2008). Internal organizational characteristics that can contribute to the centrality of behavioral bias include employee satisfaction, employee commitment, employee motivation, employee training and development, and aligning the values of the organization and the individual (Bontis & Serenko, 2009).

Credit union leadership practices seem to reflect ideas from many different leadership theories. These leadership theories include path-goal, transactional, transformational, leader-member exchange, situational, and servant. While leaders within the credit union industry often build leader and follower relationships based on a shared vision (Centini, 2005), the most common leadership practice used by credit union leaders is transformational (Colbert, Kristof-Brown, & Barrick, 2006).

Transformational leaders, as described by Burns (1978), motivate followers to commit to a higher ideal or goal, but not out of self-interest. Such leaders are traditionally characterized as charismatic, inspirational, capable of stimulating others intellectually, and capable of individualized concern for others (Defee, Esper, & Mollenkopf, 2009; Deng & Gibson, 2009). The effectiveness of transformational leaders is their ability to unite followers and change followers' goals and beliefs, represent a future vision to followers, and motivate subordinates to perform beyond expectations (Beugré, Acar, & Braun, 2006). Credit union leaders who demonstrate transformational leadership practices have increased goal agreement with followers, improved management and credit union performance, and created an environment in which followers believe they can exceed performance standards (Colbert, Kristof-Brown, & Barrick, 2006).

History of the 2008 financial crisis. Some economists consider the financial crisis of 2008 to be one of the worst economic disasters in more than 75 years (Altman, 2009). Nearly every domestic and global economic indicator has decreased. Many theorists agree that the cause of the economic crisis was rapid expansion of subprime mortgage lending and the sale of speculative subprime investment instruments (Gorton, 2008). The increase in subprime mortgage lending and the sale of subprime investment instruments contributed to a breakdown in the American credit and mortgage system that, in turn, led to the current recession (Haro & Sullivan, 2009).

Subprime mortgages are mortgages that possess higher interest rates, when compared to standard prime mortgages, balloon payments, pre-payment penalties, and excessive fees. Subprime mortgages gained in popularity in 1994 due to the introduction of new credit scoring techniques (Johnson & Neave, 2008). These new credit scoring techniques, and the decreasing of mortgage interest rate pricing indexes, helped to increase the value of subprime lending to $625 billion in 2005, from $35 billion in 1994 (Quercia, Stegman, & Davis, 2007). Individuals with a subprime mortgage were sensitive to changes in economic conditions and were likely to default on their loans when pressure on personal income increased (Quercia, Stegman, & Davis, 2007). To increase financial profitability, financial institutions packaged subprime loans into asset-backed securities and sold these securities on the open market. Bought worldwide, these subprime asset-backed securities were mixed with traditional mortgage backed securities, thus hiding the true potential risks of these investments (Bordo, 2007; Cassell & Hoffmann, 2009; Woods, Humphrey, Dowd, & Liu, 2009).

The trend continued, with subprime losses estimated to reach $200 to $300 billion (Ahmadi, Kuhle, & Varshney, 2010). Many investors worldwide purchased these securities and were unaware of the true potential risks of these investments (Bordo, 2007).

The stock market crash of 1987 established the groundwork for the financial crisis of 2008, specifically with the trading of derivatives (Baigent & Massaro, 2009; Marks, 2008). Derivatives are financial contracts that calculate value based on the worth of another asset, such as specific stocks, stock market indexes, loans, or other forms of credit (Baigent & Massaro, 2005; Gerding, 2009). Leading up to the stock market crash of 1987, overvalued derivatives were widely sold to investors and contained significant risks if the assets pledged lost value. Reacting to domestic and international monetary fluctuations, derivatives began to lose value and investors began selling. Within a few days, the stock market had fallen by 10% (Baigent & Massaro, 2005). Although considered one of the leading causes of the 1987 stock market crash, derivatives remained unregulated within the financial markets (Baigent & Massaro, 2009).

During the mid-1990s and early 2000, many financial institutions and investment firms were experiencing unprecedented levels of liquidity. Financial institutions and investment firms sought investment opportunities for excess liquidity. The derivatives market became a popular investment opportunity because of the high rates of return and the perception of low risk (Weitzner & Darroch, 2009). In March 1999, Federal Reserve Chairman Alan Geenspan argued that the derivative market should remain unregulated and, in 2000, the Commodities Futures Modernization Act allowed banks to continue to self-regulate derivatives (Marks, 2008). In reaction to a housing boom, banks began transforming mortgage derivatives into collateralized debt obligations (CDOs) by mixing traditional mortgage lending with new sub-prime lending (Hall, 2008). To make the collateralized debt obligations more appealing to investors, banks and investment firms obtained credit ratings from credit rating agencies such as Fitch, Moody's, and Standard and Poor's. These credit agencies would rate collateralized debt obligations based on a grading scale that ranged from AAA, AA, A, BBB, BB, B, CCC, CC, C, DDD, DD, and D, with AAA being the best quality. Most collateralized debt obligations, including those obligations backed by traditional and subprime mortgages, were routinely granted

AAA ratings by the credit rating agencies (Mainelli, 2008). Many of the credit rating agencies had a conflict of interest when assigning a credit risk (Mainelli, 2008). Several credit-granting methodologies were flawed and purchasers of collateralized debt obligations were incapable of identifying the high levels of risk resulting from the increase in subprime mortgages (Mainelli, 2008).

Subprime lending popularity continued to grow, reaching an all time high in 2006. An analysis by Credit Suisse revealed that 80% of all subprime lending decisions occurred with little to no documentation, loan-to-value rations often exceeded 90%, and most sub-prime loans consisted of second mortgages (Johnson & Neave, 2008). By July 2007, mortgage delinquencies began to emerge and the collateralized debt obligations market began to decline.

The current financial crisis. The first major financial disruption concerning collateralized debt obligations occurred on July 17, 2007 when two of Bear Stern's investments lost more than $20 billion in mortgage related debt (Marks, 2008). The next day, Federal Reserve Chairman Ben Bernanke indicated that an increased risk associated with collateralized debt obligations and mortgage delinquencies could influence other financial markets worldwide, and in August 2007, the Federal Reserve began lowering the discount rate, a trend that continued for months (Marks, 2008).

From August 2007 to March 2008, many financial institutions and investment firms continued to experience unprecedented losses related to collateralized debt obligations. Bear Stearns became one of the first major investment firms to identify bankruptcy as a strategic option. To avoid bankruptcy, the Federal Reserve assumed more than $30 billion of Bear Stearns liabilities and structured a merger with JPMorgan Chase (Allen & Snyder, 2009). By August 2008, the United States Treasury seized control of Fannie Mae and Freddie Mac, the two largest government sponsored mortgage security agencies (Aalbers, 2009). By September 2008, Washington Mutual Bank neared collapse and purchased by JPMorgan Chase (Wong, 2009). On October 3, 2008, Congress passed a $700 billion bailout bill designed to provide liquidity to troubled financial institutions, and increased deposit share insurance from $100,000 to $250,000 (Allen & Snyder; Marks, 2008).

That same day, Wells Fargo Bank bought failing Wachovia Bank for about $15 billion (Marks, 2008).

Through the remainder of 2008 and into the first quarter of 2009, the United States Treasury and Congress continued to take reactive measures to limit the financial crisis (Brewer & Marie, 2010). Many sectors of the economy, including the financial industry, retailers, and the automobile sector, continued to experience credit events that influenced organizational sustainability (Mazumder & Ahmad, 2010). These events included increased mortgage defaults, declining home values, liquidity and credit concerns, and financial market instability (Mazumder & Ahmad, 2010).

History of chaos theory. Historically, chaos theory has been a mathematical theory, developed for the analysis and modeling of complex dynamical systems (Gessler, 2007). Contributors to the formation and propagation of chaos theory include Lorenz (1963), Gleick (1987), Bums (2002), and Wheatley (2006). Through their work, they have developed a framework for future exploration of the possibilities and opportunities for the application of chaos theory in the social and behavioral sciences.

Attempting to understand weather patterns, Lorenz (1963) asserted that deterministic systems that evolve through phases of instability produce new nonlinear relationships. After further analysis, Lorenz popularized the "butterfly effect" which, for many, is the hallmark of chaos theory. The concept calls attention to physical and social systems of having "dependency or sensitivity to initial conditions" (Perla & Carifio, 2005, p. 269). Lorenz published these findings in a paper titled *Deterministic Non-periodic Flow* in 1963 (Lablans & Oerlemans, 2006). In this paper, Lorenz argued that non-periodic solutions are unstable, with regard to small adjustment, resulting in contrary initial states that can change into different states. His models revolutionized the forecasting and understanding of weather patterns worldwide (Lablans & Oerlemans).

The inquiry into sensitivity to initial conditions that produce different outcomes led Lorenz to believe that minor local disruptions could alter the direction of future events (Sun & Scott, 2005). Credited with identifying, mathematically, that chaos is present in everyday life experiences; Lorenz is a pioneer of chaos theory (Ng, 2009). Lorenz theorized that uncertainties, unpredictability, and nonlinear dynamics could occur within other systems, besides weather patterns (Stapleton, Hanna, & Ross, 2006). Lorenz concluded that chaos could occur within any system that is susceptible to variations of disorder caused by internal or external environmental changes (Ng, 2009). For the next several years, discussions of chaos theory remained mathematical and technical (Bums, 2002) and did not become a part of social science discourse until Gleick's (1987) publication, *Chaos: Making a New Science.* Lauser (2010) credited Gleick with transforming the work of Lorenz into broader applications of chaotic dynamics and complexity theory.

Gleick (1987) argued that in almost all interactions between humans, humans to nature, and nature to humans, patterns emerge. Despite the complexity these interactions may form, they follow three basic rules. The first rule is that an event is not capable of exact replication, second, the event can produce nonlinear outcomes, and finally the event is not predictable (Wycisk, McKelvey, & Hulsmann, 2008). Gleick argued that where activity is chaotic, the system may never repeat the same behavior more than once, but upon bounding the activity within a representational field, the behavior becomes a strange attractor. A strange attractor is a system that never settles at a fixed-point and is always moving (Bums, 2002).

These representational fields, or strange attractors, occur when behavior becomes random within a certain pattern (Dyck, Caron, & Aron, 2006). Gleick (1987) believed that randomness occurs within a certain patterns, arguing that a butterfly wing's flap causing a tornado is random, but still occurs within a weather pattern. The number of attractors determines the patterns of chaotic events within a random system. An increase in the number of attractors intensifies the unpredictability of the behavior within the system (Benbya & McKelvey, 2006). The concept of strange attractor has led to the identification of three zones of organizational action: the zone of stability, the zone of strange attractor, and the zone of randomness.

Organizations operate within three different zones, each of which can occur at any moment. The first zone is the zone of stability, in which the organization is sheltered from external changes (Bums, 2002). The second zone is the zone of strange attractor, in which the organization remains bound to the purpose, vision, and core values of the organization (Bums, 2002). The third zone is the zone of randomness, in which chaos occurs (Bums, 2002). Within the zone of strange attractor, organizational leaders attempt to reorganize and discover new ways to express purpose, vision, and core values with internal and external stakeholders and never settle at a fixed-point (Bums, 2002). The zone of strange attractor can cause unpredictable actions by organizational leaders and stakeholders (Potocan & Mulej, 2009).

If a busy street intersection has an increase in the number of auto accidents, caused by drivers ignoring the stoplight when it turns red, the municipality may install red light cameras. Drivers begin to use alternative routes to avoid red light cameras, thus decreasing sales activities for nearby businesses. The decrease in sales activity is an unpredictable response. The decreased sales activity forces leaders to discover new ways to express purpose, vision, and core values to increase sales activity. The zone of randomness is different from the zone of stability because within the zone of randomness leaders have yet to make sense of chaotic behavior to help identify opportunities. Once the organization has re-defined the zone of the strange attractor and the zone of randomness, the organization reestablishes a new zone of stability, using the experiences of the chaotic events.

The strange attractor becomes the constant within the organization. Within the strange attractor, the organization's core values exist. If leaders change or abandon the strange attractor, then leaders should establish a new zone of stability. These zones rarely perform independently. If leaders operate any of the zones independently, the organization experiences a single loop environment. A single loop environment occurs when leaders focus on the events of one zone, but is unaware of the larger environment (Bums, 2002). If the environment suddenly changes, leaders may not be able to respond to new demands (Bums, 2002). Double loop systems occur when leaders focus on a particular zone but are also aware of the environment.

Successful leadership is important to the accomplishments of any organization. Successful leadership practices are dynamic, and include three concepts: self, followers, and the organization (Crossan, Vera, & Nanjad, 2008). Organizational capability, operational intelligence, innovation and performance, and strategic intelligence support these three concepts. How leaders experience these concepts is dependent on an organizational atmosphere that is not rigid, allows the organization to experience reform, and potentially develop new values (Carr-Chellman et al., 2008). These concepts, represented in the ratchet effect model, can be slow, rapid, or instant (Hames, 2007).

Bums (2002) work builds on the past efforts of Gleick (1987) by discussing how organizations may benefit from abandoning old linear leadership paradigms by recognizing and embracing the concept of the strange attractor. Bums argued that the role of good leadership is not to make things stable, but try to make sense of chaotic behavior and to identify opportunities (Fitzpatrick, 2007). One way to help leaders make sense of chaotic behavior is to understand how the strange attractor phenomenon exists within an organization.

Current applications of chaos theory. Chaos within an organization has a way of appearing quickly and without warning. The environment organizations perform in is becoming more complex, and leaders are becoming entrenched in the day-to-day pressures of the organization (Mason, 2007). Leaders should become more aware of the order and disorder found within their organizations, rather than being surprised by sudden chaos (Mason, 2007).

The field of leadership studies is changing, with the development of new specialties within the many academic disciplines that touch on issues of leadership. With growing interest in general systems theory, cybernetics, and chaos theory social scientists are unsure how chaos theory can contribute to a viable leadership theory, if at all. An increasing number of social scientists are experimenting with nonlinear concepts (Wheatley, 2006). As organizational challenges occur, the challenge of nonlinear behavior may most likely continue into the future, until corrected. Wheatley (2006) stated, "The science of the seventeenth century cannot explain what we are challenged by in the twenty-first century" (p. 161). Leader's attempt to apply chaos theory to an analysis of organizational management has some management philosophers encouraging leaders to recognize the importance of remaining responsive to the ever-changing demands of internal and external environments (Bums, 2002). Bums (2002) believes that introducing chaos theory into organizational leadership has become a new approach to leadership psychology and philosophy, promising to transform leadership and management theories.

Because the application of chaos theory as a leadership model is new to the business environment, a gap exists in the research-based literature available to leaders interested in understanding the opportunities chaos theory might provide an organization. Most of the literature on chaos theory that does exist was focused on how chaos theory can help leaders manage the relationship between chaotic events and leadership practices (Gharajedaghi, 2005). Bums (2002), Gharajedaghi (2005), Wheatley (2006), and Mason (2007) seem to see chaos theory as a heuristic leadership paradigm, which gives emphasis to the importance of sensitivity to early conditions.

Leaders can employ chaos theory as a sensitizing model for improving decision-making (Samli, 2006). During periods of organizational chaos, leaders often process a large amount of information, which can include financial, market, and operational. Today, much of this information tends to originate from changing technology, global competition, the power structure of the organization, and the changing lifestyles of consumers. The information leaders' process can include many of these points, or only a few, but either way, leaders may benefit from the successful processing of information during chaotic events (Gharajedaghi, 2005).

Communication technology is becoming a major asset to organizations. The data stored, processed, and recovered is often at the core of the operation. Disruptions to technology, either internal or external, can quickly send the organization into chaos. Disaster recovery planning may help leaders identify how to respond to disruptions in technology. Chaos is likely to occur when the zone of randomness replaces the zone of stability. Technology is one of the most remarkable forces propelling an organization into chaos (Samli, 2006), especially as organizations become more global. Through technology, users of services are able to access information abroad. Globalization has accelerated the flow of information (Samli, 2006), and applying the concepts of chaos theory within the perspective of globalization can benefit the organization by strengthening the organization's strange attractor.

Competitive profiles of a marketplace can change at any time (Samli, 2006). Competition and marketplaces often operate in the zone of randomness that presents unique challenges. As the marketplace changes, leaders should act quickly to return the organization to the zone of stability. During the period of chaos, leaders should recognize that the current state of chaos might demand a redesign, to improve product potency (Gharajedaghi, 2005).

The speed at which change occurs can quickly create nonlinear dynamics within an organization. During a period of chaos, the change may occur at a faster rate than leaders and followers are able to comprehend (Guastello, 2008; Samli, 2006). During chaotic events that result in rapid changes, the changes can influence the development of leaders and followers. Key areas of skill development that may be challenged include identifying organizational consistency (Jalonen & Lonnqvist, 2009), innovative methods, identification of higher quality resources, and better control of resources (Barber & Warn, 2005) that help leaders return the organization to the zone of stability. The speed at which leaders react to change can challenge new product development, hasten product life cycles, and consumers' time awareness (Samli, 2006).

Complexity and paradox are the outcomes of leaders' decisions when faced with chaotic technology, competition, and the speed at which change occurs (Samli, 2006). Complexity and paradox occurs when the organization enters the zone of strange attractor, thus leaving the zone of randomness and reemerging in the newly created zone of stability (Bums, 2002). As leaders re-emerge into the newly created zone of stability, the strange attractor may also change. Leaders should identify if the purpose and values of the organization match the newly created zone of stability (Bums, 2002).

During periods of chaotic events, leaders may need to deal with all or a few of the major forces that create nonlinear dynamics within an organization. As leaders attempt to transition their organization from the zone of randomness back to the zone of stability, three additional forces could be considered. These forces include changes in the power structure, changes in lifestyles, and changes in the size of the workplace. These forces do not occur independently of changes in global competition, technology, and speed, but simultaneously.

The power structure of the organization is important when dealing with chaotic events. The power structures can encompass internal or external structures. Internal structures include the reflexive, collective consciences, and the social functions of the leadership structure within an organization (Pees, Shoop, & Ziegenfuss, 2009). As leaders within an organization experience the zone of strange attractor, leaders should contend with developing efficient teams (Dolan, Garcia, & Auerbach, 2003). External power structures can include the possibility of organizational mergers. Leaders unable to deal effectively with the zone of randomness may subject the organization to the possibility of a merger with another organization (Kavanagh & Ashkanasy, 2006). If the organization survives the zone of randomness, the leadership power structure adapts as the organization transitions through the zone of strange attractor.

Changing lifestyles of consumers are transitioning organizations into the zone of randomness with increase use of technology, shifting buying habits, and service expectations (Samli, 2006). The changing lifestyles of consumers are often the cause of chaos in many markets (Samli, 2006). Leaders often experience the need to redevelop the strange attractor of the organization to meet the demands of the changing lifestyles. As leaders redefine the strange attractor, the speed of adaptation of product innovations, and product variety become the main concerns (Reinstaller & Sanditov, 2005).

Changes in the size and composition of the labor force are the cause of chaos in many organizations (Samli, 2006). Such chaos is the result of leaders either downsizing labor to cut costs, an influx of new talented labor that is increasing operating costs, or the generation of new products and services (Bloch, 2005; Samli, 2006). As leaders become familiar with the chaotic conditions, they learn to take advantage of zone of randomness and the redeveloping of the strange attractor.

Chaos theory has potential as a consciousness-raising theoretical model for enhancing decision-making (McKenna & Martin-Smith, 2005; Samli, 2006). Leaders whom understand new technologies, globalization, and competition can assist followers with navigating through organizational chaos. The information leaders need to process may include the outcomes of their decisions, signals from the power structure of the organization, data descriptive of the changing lifestyles of consumers, and feedback from downsizing the workforce.

To understand and manage chaos in an organization, leaders should identify the behavior patterns of the strange attractor. Both the organization's purpose and its values are found within the strange attractor (Bums, 2002). A strange attractor is an organization's mission, vision, and purpose statements that represent what the organization is and wants to become. As long as the organization stays bound to its mission, vision, and purpose, or is willing to create new mission, vision, and purpose statements in response to the zone of randomness, the strange attractor can help leaders with creative decisions that establishes a new zone of stability. Organizations that operate in the zone of stability are sheltered from external changes because leadership behavior is predictable, controlled, and stable (Bums, 2002). However, if leaders ignore activity within the external environment, they can be surprised when external changes overpower predictable, controlled, and stable leadership practices that result in an organizational crisis. The financial crisis of 2008 is an example of how leaders in many sectors of the economy, financial, retailers, and automobile, became overpowered with rapid changes in the external environment. As a result, many leaders had to abandon the sheltered protection the zone of stability can provide, creating a crisis for many organizations (Mazumder & Ahmad, 2010).

During a crisis, the leader of an organization has two important tasks. The first task is to identify the purpose and values of the organization (Dolan, Garcia, & Auerbach, 2003). The second task is to determine whether challenges to the strange attractor are the cause of chaos (Bums, 2002). If the cause of change is associated with chaotic events, then the events are unforeseeable and predicting the direction of the strange attractor becomes impossible until leaders understand the relationship between the organization and the environment (Dolan, Garcia, & Auerbach, 2003).

Organizational chaos creates many challenges for leaders. The main challenge is leaders' ability to manage followers. People tend to follow blindly, even if their conformity leads in the wrong direction (Clegg, Kornberger, & Pitsis, 2005). Chaos can create opportunities for leaders to lead in the wrong direction, with followers closely behind. To find clarity in such an unclear environment, leaders should recognize whether the chaos is truly chaos or merely organizational complexity.

Organizations typically pass through periods of stability, chaos, self-organization, and stability (Dolan, Garcia, & Auerbach, 2003). As the organization passes through these periods, their leaders should try to ask and answer two questions: Is the strange attractor defining the chaos or is the chaos defining the strange attractor, was the event unforeseeable? The chaotic event may be happening so fast that, leaders may not be aware that the system is moving (Dolan, Garcia, & Auerbach, 2003).

During periods of chaos, leaders can help the organization survive by abandoning traditional management practices (Dolan, Garcia, & Auerbach, 2003). When dealing with chaos the complexity of the organization grows, leaders and followers, especially leaders, can benefit from four chaos survival essentials. These essentials include quality and customer orientation, professional autonomy and responsibility, transformational leaders instead of bosses, flatter, more agile, organization structures (Dolan, Garcia, & Auerbach, 2003).

Customers are likely to respond positively when the relationship between the organization and the customer has value (Macintosh, 2007). Maintaining customer value during chaos requires having customer-oriented employees who emphasize customer relationships (Macintosh, 2007). The consequence of not reinforcing the customer value relationship during chaos is the deepening of chaos within the organization.

Chaos within an organization can cause stress between leaders and followers (Dolan, Garcia, & Auerbach, 2003). A leader's professional autonomy and responsibility can limit the stress and allow for enhanced teamwork within the organization. The leader's professional autonomy and responsibility can also improve innovation and allow leaders and followers to articulate their own values and translate those values into creative initiatives (Dolan, Garcia, & Auerbach, 2003).

Organizations operating in the zone of randomness may benefit from transformational leaders. Transformational leaders become facilitators, thus they may ensure performance during times of chaos (Dolan, Garcia, & Auerbach, 2003). During times of organizational stress, transformational leaders advocate rational inspiration that empowers employees (Murphy, 2005).

During chaotic events, leaders should create a more flat, agile organization structure (Dolan, Garcia, & Auerbach, 2003). A flat, agile organization structure allows leaders and followers to suspend organizational bureaucratic organizational structure (Dolan, Garcia, & Auerbach, 2003), as bureaucratic structures complicate the ability of leaders to guide the organization from the zone of randomness to the zone of stability. Leaders in flat, agile organizations can establish dynamic systems, in which bottom-up structures emerge to increase long-term organization viability (Osborn & Hunt, 2007) and reestablishes a zone of stability.

Much current literature on chaos theory in the business leadership community focuses on understanding and managing chaos within organizations. No research-based literature was found that reported on how individual leaders define the experience of chaos. The current literature that does draw on chaos theory has been focused on the organization, not leaders. The published research did not include any documentation about leaders within credit unions defining or experiencing chaos.

The question of whether chaos theory could prove useful in the field of leadership studies is very much open and subject to controversy. Certainly, social scientists' abuse of importations of concepts and theoretical models from the natural sciences should cause leaders to take any exploration with caution. The warning should extend to the application of chaos theory to social organizations. Organizations face an increasingly complex external environment. Organizations themselves, as well as leadership roles, are becoming more complex. An application of systems theory may help increase the understanding of such complexity.

History of systems theory. Systems theory is widely used within organizations to help understand organizational complexity. The use of systems theory helps leaders appreciate how chaordic systems thinking influences organizational mechanics, learning management, and organizational sustainability (Putnik, 2009). Hock, former CEO of Visa, developed chaordic system thinking in 1993 as a way to describe organizational environments that are both chaotic and ordered (Hock, 1999). Chaordic systems is defined as systems that allow leaders to have an increased level of consciousness, connectivity, dissipation, indeterminacy, and emergence that assists with achieving organizational sustainability (Putnik, 2009). Leaderships' ability to self-organization and being adaptive promotes internal and external cooperation and competition (Hock, 1999). Chaordic systems thinking consist of five characteristics, which include consciousness, connectivity, indeterminacy, dissipation, and emergence (Putnik, 2009). These five characteristics help organizational systems relate with each other. The evolution of systems theory has focused on how independent organizational systems can, when influenced by chaotic events, result in a reorganization of the organization, and increase the effectiveness of leadership practices.

Developed more than 40 years ago by Ludwig von Bertalanffy, systems theory may serve as an alternative to existing organizational theories that focus on isolated unidirectional organizational relations (Kramer, 2007). Von Bertalanffy argued that organizations are open systems that have certain universal characteristics (Kramer, 2007). These characteristics include hierarchical structures, the use of energy from external environments to support sustainability, being partially bound by internal and external exchanges, self-regulations, and the capacity of reaching a final state of operations by changes based on emerging conditions (Davidson & Rowe, 2009).

Prigogine argued that systems theory could explain how chaotic events influence deterministic nonlinear systems within an organization (Svensson, Wood, & Mathisen, 2008). Prigogine believed that when internal or external events occur within an organization, the potential for unpredictable behavior increases (Svensson, 2009). The transition from old norms to new norms can strain an organization. A bifurcation point is the moment at which leaders within the organization should choose which path could most influence organizational sustainability. A bifurcation point consists of divergent, abrupt, and discontinuous changes in the system that forces leaders to choose an organizational direction that can increase organizational sustainability (Zhong & Low, 2009). When faced with making a decision at the bifurcation point, leaders could face the possibility that their organization may respond in one of five different ways (Svensson et al., 2008):

1. The old norms may dominate and systems may retreat to a previous state,
2. Newly emerging systems may dominate and the systems may begin to stabilize,
3. Systems may compete for equal attention, create tension, and oscillate between new and old,
4. The systems may create additional bifurcation points and generate confusion, until the systems settle, or
5. The systems could never settle, creating a continuous loop of unstable patterns.

Building on Prigogine's (1984) and Gleick's (1987) work, Kauffman (1993) recognized that system complexity occurs on the edge of order and chaos (Backstrom, 2009). Kauffman argued that organizations could identify and react to system complexity through four principles. These principles include, first, complex systems are at risk when maintaining equilibrium, as equilibrium does not support organization sustainability; second, complex systems have the capacity to self-organize and emerge stronger when experiencing chaotic events; third, complex systems tend to move toward the edge of chaos and fourth, complex systems cannot be managed, only disturbed (French, 2009). Kauffman further theorized that interactions among systems mainly occur during organizational change. Kauffman argued that, to facilitate the interaction between systems, interaction processes consist of repeatable, recursive, and multiplicative behaviors (Salem, 2008). During the interaction process, self-organization occurs and produces new strategies that support organizational sustainability (Salem, 2008).

Current systems theory applications. Today, systems theory is increasingly used to describe organizations. Classified as complex systems, organizations often contain various sub-systems (Samoilenko, 2008). Each sub-system has unique behaviors that could react to chaotic events differently. Understanding how these behaviors influence organizational sustainability has recently become increasingly important. To help leaders understand behavioral reactions of followers to chaotic events Kiel (1997), Senge (2006), and Holland (1995) have argued that managing behavior during chaotic events should become an essential management requirement. Leaders can benefit from three characteristics: the ability to manage the behaviors of chaotic events, which includes understanding nonlinearity, the ability to recognize organizational system sensitivity to initial conditions, and sensitivity to how non-average behavior can be a source of change (Samoilenko, 2008).

Many management philosophers have argued that both chaos and systems theory model the organizationally complexity (Das & Kumar, 2010; Goldman, Plack, Roche, Smith, & Turley, 2009; Lauser, 2010). The reason for combining systems theory and chaos theory is that systems theory focuses on the "spontaneous emergence of organization and the interface between order and chaos" (Wheelan, 2005, p. 202). Because chaos theory and systems theory are still emerging as possible leadership theories, the question of their relationship is still open to debate. The view that seems to be emerging in the literature is that chaos theory and systems theory are commonly associated with theoretical work on managing organizational change, and with the continuous themes of managing vision, communication, and organizational resistance (Palmer & Dunford, 2008).

Common Leadership Theories

Historically, several schools of thought within the field of leadership studies, each of which offers a model of implicit or explicit leadership behavior, attempt to explain how organizational systems can operate at optimal performance through a variety of leadership theories. These theories include path-goal, transactional, transformational, leader-member exchange, situational, and servant leader models of leadership theory and practice. Because one or more of these leadership theories may have heuristic value in the interpretation of the data obtained in the research study, the literature review concludes with a brief review of each.

Path-Goal theory. The path-goal leadership theory, developed by House (1971), argues that the objective of leadership is to help followers reach their goals by providing leadership direction and support (Fukushige & Spicer, 2007, Yiing & Ahmad, 2009). Leaders often help followers identify a particular path that supports organizational and individual goals by developing a rewards system before followers achieve established goals. Both the leader and follower develop a definition of the reward system, which can include monetary compensation, promotions in rank, or access to new knowledge that builds individual character. House (1971) argued that the effectiveness of achieving goals and receiving rewards was based on leadership behaviors that motivated the follower to learn skills (Stoker, 2008). The benefits of the path-goal theory are to involve followers in the decision-making process by identifying individual paths for success. A potential problem with the path-goal theory is that followers may need structure and guidance from leaders to perform the desired tasks (Yukl, 2006).

Transactional theory. Using this transactional theory, developed by Burns (1978), argued that leaders build leader and follower relationships based on contingent rewards, active management by exception, and passive management by exception (Xirasagar, 2008). Transactional leaders use contingent rewards to encourage follower behavior that focuses on performance expectations. If the follower meets these performance expectations, the leader offers a verbal or tangible reward (Xirasagar, 2008). Active management by exception helps leaders identify performance deviations and leaders provide practical solutions to the follower, which prevents problems from occurring (Burns, 1978).

Transformational theory. Transformational leaders, as described by Burns (1978), motivate followers to commit to a higher goal that is not based on their self-interest. Followers have traditionally classified transformational leaders as charismatic, inspirational, capable of stimulating others intellectually, and capable of individualized concern for others (Defee, Esper, & Mollenkopf, 2009). The effectiveness of transformational leaders is a consequence of their ability to unite followers and change followers' goals and beliefs, to represent a future vision for followers, and to motivate subordinates to perform beyond expectations (Beugré, Acar, & Braun, 2006). Burns identified two types of transformational leaders: the reformer and the revolutionary. Reformers operate on parts of the organization and a revolutionary operates on the entire organization (Beugré, Acar, & Braun, 2006). Reformers seek outcomes that are in agreement with the organization's existing trends and principles, whereas the revolutionary seeks a new direction, thus reversing existing trends and principles (Beugré, Acar, & Braun, 2006).

Leader-Member exchange theory. Graen and Scandura (1987) theorized that leader and follower relationships increase through mutually agreed upon exchanges of performance standards. Followers believe in an obligation to the organization, leaders create an environment where followers are encouraged to go beyond day-to-day performance standards, and followers are encouraged to seek experiences that are challenging (Stark & Poppler, 2009). Leaders can support the leader-member exchange theory by negotiating roles with followers. By negotiating roles, leaders and followers create an environment in which followers learn from leaders' examples, take those examples and create personalized strategies, and normalize those strategies into action plans that produce quality results (Bhal, Gulati, & Ansari, 2009).

Situational theory. In their situational leadership theory, Hershey and Blanchard drew a distinction between relationship and task behaviors (Marques, 2008). Leaders create an environment where leaders and followers choose between being tasked oriented or identifying and building relationships that increase productivity and influence organizational culture. Leaders who create an environment that focuses on task behaviors influence follower relationships by focusing on what followers should do, when followers should perform, and how followers perform (Hughes, Ginnett, & Curphy, 2002). Leaders who create an environment that focuses on building relationships influence followers by listening, facilitating, encouraging, and clarifying leader and follower roles (Hughes, Ginnett, & Curphy, 2002).

Servant leadership theory. Developed by Greenleaf in the early 1970s, servant leadership helps build leader and follower relationships through an awareness of follower actions, commitment to increasing follower skills and performance, and by trusting and empowering followers (Anderson, 2009). Servant leaders promote the development and performance of followers by practicing leadership authenticity, which includes a sincere interest in the development of followers, contributing to strengthening the organization's culture, sharing power between leader and follower, and developing leadership practices for the good of the organization, followers, and customers (Washington, Sutton, & Feild, 2006).

Conclusion

The history of credit unions, which emerged worldwide as an alternative to the traditional banking system, spans more than 170 years. The American credit union system is more than 100 years old, and today more than 7,554 federally insured credit unions serve nearly 90 million members with deposits totaling more than $752 billion (National Credit Union Administration, 2010a). Despite the size and financial importance of the credit union sector, no research-based studies of the lived experience of leading or managing credit union organizations could be found. This is also the case for the experience of leading credit unions during periods of organizational crisis associated with contractions of the national economy, even though such contractions are a predictable feature of cyclical capitalist economies. The goal of phenomenological research is to commence filling such gaps in the literature.

One of the principles of phenomenological research is that scientific investigation of subjective experience requires the interrogation of first-person recollections of life experience that are free of the presuppositions of the person doing the research. Epoche is a procedure used when the researcher sets aside all preconceived ideas (Moustakas, 1994). Once the data has been collected and analyzed, existing theoretical perspectives may be used to interpret the findings. To this end, the literature review has presented the theoretical perspectives of chaos and systems theory now under consideration within the fields of organizational development and leadership. Short descriptions of six of the more conventional leadership models of leadership practice were presented to conclude a review of theoretical literature that may prove to be of heuristic value for credit union leaders.

Chaos theory may offer unusually timely insights because of the financial crisis of 2008. The financial crisis of 2008 is one of the worst economic disasters in more than 75 years (Altman, 2009). Nearly every economic indicator has decreased, domestically and globally. The application of chaos theory to leadership behavior during a major business contraction would be new to business literature.

Summary

The general topic of the research study was the relationship between the credit crisis and recession of 2008-2010, which continues to create turmoil within the national economy and sectors of the financial industry. In response to the current recession, credit union leaders have tightened budgets, experienced decreased revenue, decreased employee compensation, deferred branch expansion, and closed branch offices, which have caused interpersonal and interdepartmental organizational chaos (Gustafson, 2009). The purpose of Chapter 2 was to provide a review of the current literature on the history of credit unions, credit union leadership practices, and the current financial crisis. Additional literature reviewed included chaos theory, systems theory, and common leadership practices.

For over 100 years, credit unions have served as an alternative to the traditional banking system, with 7,554 federally insured credit unions serving nearly 90 million members, with deposits totaling more than $752 billion (National Credit Union Administration, 2010a). Credit union leadership practices seem to reflect ideas from many different leadership theories. These leadership theories include path-goal, transactional, transformational, leader-member exchange, situational, and servant. Leaders within the credit union industry often build leader and follower relationships based on a shared vision (Centini, 2005). The most common leadership practice used by credit union leaders is transformational (Colbert, Kristof-Brown, & Barrick, 2006).

Economic crises, recessions, and depressions are not unfamiliar events in the economic history of modern nations. A review of the literature indicated that the current economic crisis was brought on by the proliferation of subprime mortgages, new credit scoring techniques, decreased mortgage interest rate pricing indexes, and the way derivatives were scored and traded (Baigent & Massaro, 2009; Marks, 2008). The speed at which change occurs can quickly create nonlinear dynamics within an organization. During a period of chaos, the change may be occurring at a faster rate than leaders and followers are able to comprehend (Guastello, 2008; Samli, 2006). During chaotic events that result in fast changes, the fast changes can increase organizational complexity. Systems theory is often used to help identify and understand organizational complexity.

Systems theory is widely used within organizations to help leaders understand organizational complexity. The use of systems theory helps leaders understand how chaordic systems thinking influences organizational mechanics, learning management, and organizational sustainability (Putnik, 2009). The evolution of systems theory has focused on how independent organizational systems interact, and how these interactions can, when influenced by chaotic events, result in a reorganization of the organization, and an increased effectiveness of leadership practices. Common leadership theories, which include path-goal, transactional, transformational, leader-member exchange, situational, and servant, often have been employed to support the use of systems theory within an organization.

The purpose of the research study was to explore the lived experiences of a purposive sample of credit union leaders and managers.

The research study builds on a review of historical, theoretical and research literature that forms the context for an investigation of the credit union leadership experience when faced with an organization-threatening recession. Chapter 3 will review the method used to conduct the research study and provides details relevant to the research design, population, sampling, confidentiality, and informed consent of research participants, data collection, validity and reliability, and data analysis.

Chapter 3
RESEARCH METHOD

The research study explored the experiences, perceptions, attitudes, and behaviors of leaders in charge of individual credit unions during a period of economic crisis and contraction. The research procedure selected was qualitative, with a phenomenological design adapted from Moustakas (1994). The main characteristic of the phenomenological approach was the use of loosely structured open-ended interviews, after which the interview transcripts were reduced to natural meanings in an attempt to capture common patterns of subjective experience. Extracted from interview data through analysis of the interview transcripts was themes and patterns of interest. The specific population used for the research study included CEOs, CFOs, vice presidents, and senior managers who influence organizational strategies and tactics in individual credit unions operating within the State of Texas. Each qualifying participant was expected to have had 10 or more years of experience within the credit union industry.

Chapter 3 opens with the identification of the research method used and the rationale for the selection. A description of research question, population, and sampling frame follows. A full discussion of the provisions for obtaining informed consent and of insuring confidentiality followed by descriptions of the research geographic location, data collection techniques to be used, instrumentation, and the measures taken to enhance the reliability and the validity of the data. Chapter 3 concludes with a detailed presentation and explanation of the phenomenological data analysis process used.

Research Method

The research method used for this study was qualitative. The primary reason for selecting a qualitative methodology for the research study was that the general research question could only be answered with qualitative data. The goal of the research was to investigate and interpret the subjective experiences of the participants, as revealed by qualitative data. The goal of the research study was to extract and capture participants' thoughts and feelings.

Qualitative research methodologies have a lengthy history, helping researchers understand phenomenon occurring within the management of complex organizations (Cassell & Symon, 2006). Qualitative procedures are appropriate when the goal of the investigation is to develop a deep understanding of the why and how a phenomenon occurs (Tonge, 2008). Qualitative research methodologies often use in-depth interviews to capture and evaluate what some describe as intangible knowledge intrinsic to social interaction (McEvoy & Richards, 2006). The task of the researcher is to evaluate intangible knowledge through interpreting participants' responses (McEvoy & Richards, 2006). Such qualitative research uses open-ended questions that allow participants to communicate their responses to the problem under discussion and to explore emergent themes during the research (Creswell, 2005; Moustakas, 1994). The general purpose of qualitative inquiry is to explore, describe, and explain phenomenon (Marshall & Rossman, 2006).

Appropriateness of Design

The design selected for data analysis was empirical phenomenological, as derived and adapted from the procedures developed by Moustakas (1994). Empirical phenomenology is an established research technique for understanding participants' experiences (Yeomans, 2008). Developed in the 1960s by van Kaam and others, empirical phenomenology "is an interactive process research process that is used to collect and distill the subjective recollections of experience using a series of data collection techniques interspersed with feedback" (Willis, 2008, p. 207).

The empirical phenomenological data analysis process allowed participants to be reflective by establishing the context of participants' experiences and constructing the meaning of those experiences (Flood, 2010). Empirical phenomenological research design was appropriate for the research study because empirical phenomenological research obtains an understanding of emerging patterns of the credit union leader's experiences. Qualitative research procedures, interviews with open-ended questions, help participants discuss their responses and to explore themes with the interviewer during the interviews (Creswell, 2005; Moustakas, 1994). The data collection technique used was that of open-ended questions with a focus on identifying a synergy of the recalled experiences and meanings of participants (Walker, 2007). The advantage of the phenomenological interviewing method was the interviewer's ability to remain flexible and responsive to the direction of the interview without a predetermined outcome about the phenomenon (Patton, 2002). The interviews were conducted as an interactive processes to collect data from targeted participants, using a series of data collection procedures (Willis, 2008), which included collecting the original data through naïve descriptions, open-ended questions, and active dialogue with the participants describing their experiences. The transcripts of the interviews were enriched through reflective analysis and interpretation of the responses to open-ended questions and dialogue (Moustakas, 1994).

Research Questions

A protocol of open-ended interview questions assisted the interviewer in eliciting complete and truthful recollections of the participants' experience of crisis and response. The general and primary research question for the research study was: *How did the top leaders of certain individual credit unions experience the credit crisis and recession of 2008-2010?* Secondary questions helped understand how top leaders of credit union leaders experienced, perceived, interpreted, and reacted to the credit crisis and recession of 2008-2010. Secondary research questions assisted in understanding the lived experiences of the research participants and guided the collection of data. The secondary research questions included:

1. When and how did you first notice the external environmental changes that threatened your organization? What were the danger signals?
2. As the external danger signals increased, what were the first signals of internal dysfunction?
3. How would you describe your perceptions of and feelings about the external and internal situations you found yourself confronted with?
4. How would you describe your emotional and cognitive responses to the external and internal events you were required to deal with?
5. If you have not already done so, would you use the word chaos to describe any aspect of your experiences over the past two years?
6. Using hindsight, were your responses as timely and/or as creative as needed?

Population

The population for the research study was that of credit union leaders, defined as CEOs, vice presidents, and senior managers who influenced strategy development, and employed within the 559 credit unions located in the State of Texas (CU Data, 2010) at the time of the interviews. To qualify for participation, a credit union leader should have had 10 or more years of experience within the credit union industry. Purposive selection assisted with the selection of the 12 participants within three geographic locations around the State of Texas. The geographic locations are the metropolitan areas of Austin, Dallas, and Houston. As of May 2010, the Austin geographic location contained 24 credit unions; the Dallas geographic location, 61 credit unions; and the Houston geographic location, 108 credit unions (CU Data, 2010).

Sampling Frame and Geographic Location

The sampling method used in this research study was purposive sampling. The intent of purposive sampling is identifying and using as participants, the most cooperative, experienced, and articulate leaders within the studied population (Barbour, 2001). The objective of using a purposive sample is to find the best informants possible with which to identify the phenomena, themes, and within the themes the patterns of experience that are of interest to the investigator (Denzin & Lincoln, 2005). Twelve credit union leaders, holding the position of senior manager or higher and influenced strategy development with 10 or more years of experience within the credit union industry, volunteered as participants in the research study.

Confidentiality and Informed Consent

To protect the confidentiality and privacy of the individuals participating in this study, information about voluntary participation was provided to each individual prior to the start of the research and after receiving University Institutional Review Board (IRB) approval. All interviews were recorded, without using participants' names or any identifiers, in order to maintain confidentiality during the research study. Confidentiality and informed consent are important when conducting research using human subjects. Confidentiality allows participants to engage in interactive research without fear of judgment, isolation from other research participants, and interference from other participants (Magi, 2008). Most importantly, confidentiality protects the privacy of the participant.

Instrumentation

The most common method used in qualitative research is face-to-face interviews (Couch & McKenzie, 2006). Researchers employ qualitative research methods when a lack of research in a specific field dictates the need for an exploratory study (Mason & Staude, 2009). Strength of qualitative research procedures is that it allows participants to discuss their responses and to explore themes with the interviewer during the interview (Creswell, 2005; Moustakas, 1994). Since intensive and open-ended interviewing can encourage interaction between researcher and subject, qualitative research may allow for immediate exploration of emerging themes (Breakwell, 2004).

Qualitative research involves interviewing participants to identify themes in the form of words. The words collected, the data, emerge into two categories: interview data as resources and interview data as topics. Interview data as resources is used to reflect the participants' reality outside the interview and interview data as topics is used to reflect the participants' interactions with the researcher (Seale, Gobo, Gubrium, & Silverman, 2007). A quantitative researcher, who attempts to isolate cause and effect, lack the ability to capture individual subjective perspectives because a goal of quantitative research is to extract and measure experience, instead of studying the experience directly (Denzin & Lincoln, 2008). A qualitative research design assists with the study of experience.

The design selected for data analysis was phenomenological, as derived and adapted from the procedures developed by Moustakas (1994). The interviews were conducted as interactive processes to collect data from targeted participants, using a series of data collection procedures (Willis, 2008), which included collecting the original data through naïve descriptions, using open-ended questions, and active dialogue with the participants describing their experiences. The transcripts of the interviews were enriched through reflective analysis and interpretation of the responses to open-ended questions and dialogue (Moustakas, 1994).

Interview questions. Fourteen open-ended questions were used for the interview process to collect data relevant to the general and primary research questions, *How did the top leaders of certain individual credit unions experience the credit crisis and recession of 2008-2010?* The secondary research questions included:

1. When and how did you first notice the external environmental changes that threatened your organization? What were the danger signals?
2. As the external danger signals increased, what were the first signals of internal dysfunction?
3. How would you describe your perceptions of and feelings about the external and internal situations you found yourself confronted with?
4. How would you describe your emotional and cognitive responses to the external and internal events you were required to deal with?

5. If you have not already done so, would you use the word chaos to describe any aspect of your experiences over the past two years?
6. Using hindsight, were your responses as timely and/or as creative as needed?

The purpose of the secondary research questions was to identify how credit union leaders responded to organizational crises caused by negative changes in the general economic environment within which they operate. The decisions made by leaders can influence various internal organizational variables and the decision-making process can have far-reaching organizational sustainability implications (McKenzie, Woolf, van Winkelen, & Morgan, 2009). Additional research questions, found in Appendix B, were general questions used to identify a participant's degree of engagement within the credit union, influence, and perceptions.

Pilot study. A pilot study was necessary to test the research questions, thus lending credibility to the study instrument. Conducting a pilot study helped establish validity of the research questions and identify other research characteristics, such as the number of questions, quality of questions, question order, and participant understanding of the question, which could influence the actual study. Purposively selected to participate in the pilot study, the criterion for pilot study participation was being a credit union leader, holding the position of senior manager or higher and influenced strategy development with 10 or more years of experience within the credit union industry. Contacted by telephone and email, participants were informed about the purpose of the research, verified that he or she held the position of senior manager or higher, influenced strategy development, and had 10 or more years of experience within the credit union industry; a participant was asked if he or she was willing to participate in the research study. Once a participant agreed to participate in the pilot research study, the participant received the Informed Consent: Participants 18 Years of Age and Older form, found in Appendix A, for review and signature.

After an agreed upon date and time with all participants, the pilot study was conducted in Houston. Each participant received a research code to maintain confidentiality. The research codes consisted of

CEO-Test-1, CEO-Test-2, VP-Test-1, and VP-Test-2. Each participant returned the signed Informed Consent: Participants 18 Years of Age and Older form and were asked if he or she had any questions about the research before beginning. None of the participants had any questions. The participants were reminded that the research session would be recorded using an electronic recording device, that the electronic recording will remain confidential, that the digital audio recordings would be transcribed, and that all research data would be stored electronically, password protected, on the researcher's computer and electronically destroyed after five years. Participants were informed that they could withdrawal from the research at any time without consequences.

The pilot study provided an opportunity to evaluate the depth of open-ended questions that allow participants to communicate their responses to the problem under discussion and to explore emergent themes during the research (Creswell, 2005; Moustakas, 1994) and test the reliability of the research method. Reliability in qualitative research using a phenomenological design means that the administration of the interviews can occur several times, with the same population, and produce nearly the same results (Healy & Perry, 2000). Reliability in qualitative research using a phenomenological design also means that the criterion is trustworthy, credible, dependable, transferable, and confirmable to other industries (Bryman & Bell, 2007). The results of the pilot were the research questions were sufficient to stimulate the adequate recall of the credit union leader's experience of leadership performance during organizational crises. Feedback from the pilot study about research effectiveness resulted in two changes to the conduct of the interviews.

The first change to the research process, because of the pilot study, was small group interviews of two to four saved time and proved convenient for the subjects of the research, without changing the quality or content of the participation. The decision was made to conduct the primary research using four groups of participants. The second change to the research process was given the small group configuration and interactivity of the interviews, it became necessary to alternate between the participants who would answer interview questions first so the same participant did not set the pace by answering the question first. Data collected from the pilot study was not included in the research findings.

Data Collection

The research interviews began with the first one conducted in Houston, Texas; the second in Dallas, Texas; the third in Austin, Texas; and the fourth in Houston, Texas. Found in Appendix C is the Permission to Use Premises forms for the three research locations. Following the same pattern as with the pilot test, participants were purposively selected to participate in the study. The criterion for study participation was being a credit union leader, holding the position of senior manager or higher and influenced strategy development, with 10 or more years of experience within the credit union industry. Contacted by telephone and email, participants were informed about the purpose of the research, verified that he or she held the position of senior manager or higher, influenced strategy development, had 10 or more years of experience within the credit union industry; a participant was asked if he or she was willing to participate in the research study. Once a participant agreed to participate in the pilot research study, the participant received the Informed Consent: Participants 18 Years of Age and Older form, found in Appendix A, for review and signature. To maintain validity, each research session followed a similar protocol, which included describing in detail the purpose of the research study, describing the potential benefits of participating in the research, and reading each question in order.

Houston, Texas. After scheduling agreed upon date and time with all participants, the first research study was conducted in Houston. Each participant received a research code to maintain confidentiality. The research codes consisted of CEO-H-1, CEO-H-2, VP-H-1, and VP-H-2. Each participant returned the signed Informed Consent: Participants 18 Years of Age and Older form and were asked if he or she had any questions about the research before beginning. None of the participants had any questions. The participants were reminded that the research session would be recorded using an electronic recording device, that the electronic recording will remain confidential, that the digital audio recordings would be transcribed, and that all research data would be stored electronically, password protected, on the researcher's computer and electronically destroyed after five years. Participants were informed that they could withdrawal from the research at any time without consequences.

Dallas, Texas. The second research session took place in Dallas, Texas, after a date and time all participants agreed to. Each participant received a research code to maintain confidentiality. The research codes consisted of CEO-D-1, CEO-D-2, and SM-D-1. Each participant returned the signed Informed Consent: Participants 18 Years of Age and Older form and were asked if he or she had any questions about the research before beginning. None of the participants had any questions. The participants were reminded that the research session would be recorded using an electronic recording device, that the electronic recording will remain confidential, that the digital audio recordings would be transcribed, and that all research data would be stored electronically, password protected, on the researcher's computer and electronically destroyed after five years. Participants were informed that they could withdrawal from the research at any time without consequences.

Austin, Texas. The third research session took place in Austin, Texas, after a date and time all participants agreed to. Each participant received a research code to maintain confidentiality. The research codes consisted of CEO-A-1, CEO-A-2, and CEO-A-3. Each participant returned the signed Informed Consent: Participants 18 Years of Age and Older form and were asked if he or she had any questions about the research before beginning. None of the participants had any questions. The participants were reminded that the research session would be recorded using an electronic recording device, that the electronic recording will remain confidential, that the digital audio recordings would be transcribed, and that all research data would be stored electronically, password protected, on the researcher's computer and electronically destroyed after five years. Participants were informed that they could withdrawal from the research at any time without consequences.

Houston, Texas. The fourth research session took place in Houston, Texas, after a date and time all participants agreed to. Each participant received a research code to maintain confidentiality. The research codes consisted of CEO-H-3 and VP-H-3. Each participant returned the signed Informed Consent: Participants 18 Years of Age and Older form and were asked if he or she had any questions about the research before beginning. None of the participants had any questions. The participants were reminded that the research session would be recorded using an electronic recording device, that the electronic recording will remain confidential, that the digital audio recordings would be transcribed, and that all research data would be stored electronically, password protected, on the researcher's computer and electronically destroyed after five years. Participants were informed that they could withdrawal from the research at any time without consequences.

Time for the four interview sessions totaled 4 hours and 17 minutes. The recording times ranged from 30 minutes to 1 hour and 37 minutes, with a mean recording time of 1 hour and 4 minutes. A professional transcriptionist transcribed each recording and prepared it for analysis.

Validity and Reliability

Establishing both the validity and reliability of a phenomenological study is important if even limited generalizations about the data are to be made from the findings (Creswell, 2009). Validity focuses on the accuracy of the findings, whereas reliability focuses on replication of the research process (Sprenkle & Piercy, 2005). Factors that may influence validity and reliability of phenomenological research design may include the rapport established between the interviewer and those participating, and the consistency of the interview setting and process. In phenomenological research, the participant should trust the interviewer and should be willing to be truthful. The investigator should be willing to exercise epoche in order to set aside all presuppositions that might distort apprehension and analysis of the data (Moustakas, 1994).

Internal validity. Validity in a qualitative study is an attempt to assess the findings as described by the participants and researcher (Creswell, 2005). Internal validity is the capacity of the research instrument to perform as designed. For the research study, the research instrument is face-to-face interviews, which is the most common method used in qualitative research (Couch & McKenzie, 2006). Threats to internal validity include unexamined presuppositions that are implicit in the research environment and process, as well as research participant and researcher expectations (Schwab, 2005). The research study established internal validity through the phenomenological practice of epoche (Moustakas, 1994).

One of the principles of phenomenological research is that scientific investigation of subjective experience and the interrogation of recollections of life experience, free of the presuppositions of the person doing the research. The procedure used is called epoche, in which the researcher sets aside all preconceived ideas. Epoche is a process by which investigators sets aside all presuppositions that might distort their perceptions and interpretation of the interview data (Moustakas, 1994). To test the validity of the research study, a pilot study was conducted. The results of the pilot study identified that the research questions were sufficient to stimulate the adequate recall of the credit union leader's experience of leadership performance during organizational crises.

External validity. External validity in qualitative research, using a phenomenological design, means that the administration of the interviews can occur several times, with the same population, and produce nearly the same results (Healy & Perry, 2000). The criterion is trustworthy, credible, dependable, transferable, and confirmable to other industries (Bryman & Bell, 2007). External validity determines whether conclusions can hold externally and exist across different populations, other research settings, and in research conducted in the future (Smith & Albaum, 2005). Creswell (2005) stated that the goal of qualitative research was to study a specific circumstance, group, or setting. Transferability to other industries was considered a weakness in phenomenological research (Creswell, 2005). Duplication of qualitative studies may not produce identical results because participants' experiences and their explanations of their experiences may vary. However, the reliability of the participants should not be discounted (Creswell, 2005). The population for this research study consisted of credit union leaders, defined as CEOs, vice presidents, and senior managers who influence strategy development, and are currently employed within the credit union industry, solely located in the State of Texas. Based on these industry and geographic delimitations, the results of the research study may only be generalized to a larger population and other financial sectors with great care.

Reliability. Reliability is the consistency and dependability of the research study, meaning that repeating the measurements several times may yield the same results (Creswell, 2009). A measurement that generates inconsistent results may not be reliable and may indicate a need for a careful review of the measurement instrument (Neuman, 2003). To improve reliability in this research study, the following methods were employed, as suggested by Priest (2002):

1. Disclosing research orientation in the data collection section of chapter three,
2. Establishing an audit trail to detail how data was collected,
3. Ensuring accuracy of audio recordings and transcripts by comparing transcripts to the recordings,
4. Interpreting data through verbatim of audio transcripts and using a large blank wall to help organize the grouping of responses by assigning each major research group and responses a colored index card to visualize the data, and
5. Having concentrated engagement with the research material by becoming immersed with the data to identify meanings and themes.

Data Analysis

The details of phenomenological data analysis differ among researchers, but all have certain elements in common. Phenomenological research requires a systematic approach to the analysis of self-reported subjective data contained in the transcripts of interviews (Creswell, 2005). Phenomenological researchers seek a reliable way of identifying and deriving common themes and patterns from interview data. They use analytical processes designed to find common meanings and essences in the content of the transcripts of open-ended interviews. The phenomenologist often uses constructed narratives to present and interpret the shared experiences with common meanings and essences revealed by selected research subjects.

The analytical process used for this research is adapted from the mode of data analysis developed by Moustakas (1994) through a modification of the analytical scheme first used by van Kaam (1959, 1966). Following Moustakas, the data analysis took place in six steps:

Step 1. A reading and rereading of the statements made during each interview of each participant. This is the first examination of the raw data.

Step 2. Returning to each transcript, statements, phrases, or words that seem to be a descriptor of a subjectively significant aspect of the experience reported by each participant were highlighted.

Step 3. A list is made from each participant's transcript of all the highlighted descriptors of the participant's experiences. These are the *meaning units* of the participant's experiences of changes in the external environment and changes internal to the organization.

Step 4. Analytical process is continued by clustering the related and invariant (recurring) meaning units into *themes*. This is done for each transcript in order to identify themes that emerge in individual experience. These themes contain the recurring meanings and essences of the participant's experiences.

Step 5. After intensive examination of the meaning units and themes obtained from each participant, a narrative *description* of the experiences in question was constructed for each participant, using verbatim quotations as examples. This resulted in 12 individual, but similar descriptions (stories) of the experience, made up of meaning units (meanings) and themes (essences).

Step 6. The final step was the construction of a single universal or composite narrative of the experiences from the 12 individual descriptions that is a generalized description of the meanings and essences of the experiences for, the group as a whole.

The analytical process, adapted from the mode of data analysis developed by Moustakas (1994), helped organize reduce the raw data into preliminary grouping of statements. The reduction of the raw data into preliminary grouping allowed for phenomenological reduction and elimination, clustering and creating initial themes, final identification, and validation of the raw research to identify common themes, individual narratives using common themes, and generalizing the narratives into a composite description (Moustakas; van Kaam, 1959).

The audio recordings from each interview sessions were transcribed by a professional transcription service, which is found in Appendix D, E, F, and G. The transcripts were intensely reviewed to identify grouping of statements among the participants. Similarities in the responses to the interview questions from each session, following steps one and two of the Moustakas analytical scheme, allowed for a preliminary listing of groups for further data reduction and analysis. Placed on a large blank wall, similarities were transferred to index cards. The index cards and large blank wall helped organize the grouping of responses and each major research group was given a colored index card. A white index card indicated the research question, green index cards indicated a response was from a CEO, violet index cards indicated a response from a vice president, and a blue index card indicated a response from a senior manager. The use of a large blank wall allowed for a visual representation of the preliminary listing of statements for further reduction of data analysis, which included meaning units and themes. The visual representation of the data allowed for reflection, imaginative variation, and a portrayal of the experiences (Moustakas, 1994). The graphic display of elements of the interview transcripts assisted in identifying and isolating the significant meaning units and recurrent themes that captured the meanings and essences of the participants' recollections of perceptions and responses to complex events over a period of more than two years of financial crisis.

The method of data analysis selected is appropriate for the goals of the research study because the inquiry focuses on the subjective meanings and essences of the participants' recollections of perceptions and responses to complex events over a period of more than two years of financial crisis. The 12 lists of meaning units and themes, and the 12 individual narratives were presented as the findings of the current phenomenological research study. The composite narrative was presented as a summative finding, and with appropriate caution, as a generalized finding descriptive of the experience of credit union leaders during a period of great financial turmoil.

Summary

The purpose of this qualitative phenomenological research study was to explore the relationship between the credit crisis and recession of 2008-2010 and the lived experience of credit union leaders during that period of stress. The discussion of research procedures opened with the rationale for the decision to use a qualitative research procedure, with a phenomenological design, to collect data to capture the actual lived experiences of credit union leaders during a national recession. The general population of credit union leaders is identified, followed by the rationale for a purposive sampling procedure to be used in the Texas metropolitan areas of Austin, Dallas, and Houston. The provisions for obtaining informed consent from and insuring confidentiality for the volunteer participants in the research are outlined in detail. A discussion of the data collection technique to be used, using deep interviews with open-ended questions, is followed by a description of the measures to be taken against the threats to reliability and validity. The chapter concludes with a description of the data analysis process to be used and its basis in the van Kaam system, as modified by Moustakas (1994). Chapter 4 describes the findings obtained from the systemic analysis of the data collected from 12 interviews of credit union leaders during the financial crisis of 2008-2010.

Chapter 4

RESULTS

The purpose of the research was to explore the experiences, perceptions, attitudes, and behaviors of leaders in charge of individual credit unions during a period of economic crisis and contraction specifically the financial crisis of 2008 and ensuing recession. The research procedure selected was qualitative, with a phenomenological design adapted from Moustakas (1994). Participants were CEOs and vice presidents who influenced organizational strategies and tactics in individual credit unions operating within the State of Texas. Each qualifying participant had 10 or more years of experience within the credit union industry. The participants who responded were interviewed using open-ended questions that allowed them to recall and reflect on their experience of the crisis under investigation and to explore emergent themes with the investigator during the research (Creswell, 2005; Moustakas, 1994). The general purpose of qualitative inquiry is to explore, describe, and explain the phenomenon of subjective experience (Marshall & Rossman, 2006). The phenomenological data analysis process used established the context of participants' experiences and aided in constructing the meaning of those experiences (Flood, 2010). A phenomenological research design was appropriate for the research because it generated data that revealed the emerging patterns of credit union leader's experiences under stress.

Chapter 1 presents the background of the financial crisis, the specific problem investigated, the purpose of the study, the conceptual framework used, and the academic and social significance of the study. Chapter 2 reviewed relevant literature of the history of credit unions, credit union leadership practices, the current financial crisis, and identified gaps in the literature about credit union leadership. Chapter 2 also reviewed recent attempts to use concepts and models from chaos and systems theory for the explanation of leadership behavior in organizations under extreme stress. Chapter 3 presented the method used to conduct this research and provided details relevant to the research design, the population selected and sampled, along with issues of confidentiality and informed consent. The chapter concluded with a discussion of data collection and data analysis. The present chapter presents the research question, demographics, findings, meaning units, and common themes.

Research Questions

The use of qualitative phenomenological research approach allowed for the examination of the perceptions top leaders of certain credit unions in the state of Texas regarding the credit crisis and recession of 2008-2010. Findings from the research study may add new knowledge about leadership performance during organizational crises. A protocol of open-ended interview questions assisted the interviewer in eliciting complete and truthful recollections of the participants' experience of crisis and response. The general and primary research question answered by the research study was: *How did the top leaders of certain individual credit unions experience the credit crisis and recession of 2008-2010?*

Demographics

The population for the research study was that of credit union leaders, defined as CEOs, vice presidents, and senior managers, who influenced strategy development, and employed within the 559 credit unions located in the State of Texas (CU Data, 2010). To qualify for participation, a credit union leader should have had 10 or more years of experience within the credit union industry. The purposive sample was composed of 12 credit union leaders selected from the metropolitan areas of Austin, Dallas, and Houston. Three participants were from Austin; three from Dallas; and six from Houston. Table 2 represents the average length of credit union leadership experience by location. As of May 2010, the Austin geographic location contained 24 credit unions, the Dallas geographic location, 61 credit unions, and the Houston geographic location accounted for 108 credit unions (CU Data, 2010).

The intent of purposive sampling was to identify, the most cooperative, experienced, and articulate leaders within the population (Barbour, 2001) in order to find the best informants possible with which to identify the phenomena, themes, and patterns of experience of interest in the study (Denzin & Lincoln, 2005).

The scope of the research study was restricted to interviews with CEOs, CFOs, vice presidents, and senior managers of credit unions who influenced strategy development for their organizations. Participant leadership positions within the credit union included three CEOs from Austin, Texas, two CEOs and one senior manager from Dallas, Texas, and three CEOs and three vice presidents from Houston, Texas. Excluded from the research study was middle management, because middle managers and supervisors are not usually involved with strategy development. Participants having at least 10 years of successful leadership experience might be interested in the problem of mapping credit union leadership perceptions of and responses to the current fiscal crisis. CEOs, CFOs, vice presidents, and senior managers of credit unions represented the general population of credit union leaders and top managers were the primary decision makers responsible for the responses to the national credit crisis and recession, and have experience with the day-to-day operation of their credit unions.

Table 2 Average Years of Credit Union Experience by Geographic Location (rounded)

Geographic Location	CEO	Vice President	Senior Manager	Average
Austin, Texas	29	0	0	29
Dallas, Texas	29	0	10	22
Houston, Texas	18	15	0	16
Average	25	15	10	21

Findings

The analytical process, adapted from the mode of data analysis developed by Moustakas (1994), through a modification of the analytical scheme first used by van Kaam (1959, 1966), helped organize reduce the raw data into preliminary grouping of statements. The reduction of the raw data into preliminary grouping allowed for phenomenological reduction and elimination, clustering and creating initial themes, final identification, and validation of the raw research to identify common themes, individual narratives using common themes, and generalizing the narratives into a composite description (Moustakas, 1994; van Kaam, 1959).

Three sections incorporate the thematic representation of the data. The first section includes individual descriptions of each participant's answers to the research questions (stories), the second section includes an overview, description, and analysis of the research questions (meaning units), and the third section introduces the key themes identified within the data (themes). The entire set of expressions used by each participant during the interviews can be viewed in Appendix D for Houston, Texas, Appendix E for Dallas, Texas, Appendix F for Austin, Texas, and Appendix G for Houston, Texas.

Individual descriptions: CEO-H-1. CEO-H-1 first noticed the external environmental changes that threatened the organization when:

> Roughly about three years ago and the pricing of mortgaged back securities and how those prices at the bottom of the market fell out basically and people holding securities that were highly rated but in the values of the current market values depleted to a point where you're forced to hold on to those situations until -- until maturity. And the impact that that had was when there were downgrades to those securities.

and the danger signals were:

> Clearly the failures of the institutions. There were many reports of future job losses that were coming down, unemployment was on the rise, delinquency was on the rise. Delinquencies in particular in mortgages was where the key element was started and it was a kind of domino effect with institutions starting to fail as a result

of the accounting issues that they had to address with these mortgage-backed securities.

As the external danger signals increased, the first signs of internal dysfunction were "I think what we started to see was sometimes you might, some people might, want to overreact to the situation. Some were in denial." As the external environmental changes increased, CEO-H-1's perceptions of and feelings about the situations were anger and a desire for accountability. CEO-H-1 realized that the "...whole situation was on a global scale. Then you kind of rethink the situation and realize that it wasn't one single individual or even a group of individuals that created the environment." CEO-H-1's emotional and cognitive responses to the internal and external events included that one should "...remove your emotion from the situation so that you can be objective over the matter and how you're going to deal with the events and the circumstances that you have to deal with."

When asked whether experiences over the last couple of years could be described as chaos, CEO-H-1 replied that the experiences could be described, as "controlled chaos would be more appropriate in what has happened over the last couple of years, because I say it that [sic] chaos from a perspective of very little control over the situation." When recalling if responses were as timely and/or creative as needed CEO-H-1 stated that:

> I can't think of anything that we could have done differently or would have done differently knowing the facts today, because ultimately we came out of this thing looking, in my opinion, better than where we, when we came in.

Individual descriptions: CEO-H-2. CEO-H-2 first noticed the external environmental changes that threatened the organization when:

> The financial crisis had some very clear and significant danger signals back in September 2008 that we knew would impact our credit union here locally. As you saw major Wall Street firms like Bear Sterns and Lehman Brothers go away in a very short amount of time.

Major financial institutions like Wachovia Bank and Washington Mutual get merged into mega banks in a matter of days

and the danger signals were:

It was pretty clear that we are about to face a very serious financial situation that was going to impact us even though that's going on Wall Street. We knew the ripple effect here at Houston was going to be significant. We're very reliant as a community on oil and energy and when those kinds of activities occur, the economy slows down, you fall into recession and typically that impacts the energy sector in a negative manner.

As the external danger signals increased, the first sign of internal dysfunction was:

A state of denial regarding some major projects that we had in motion that we were out of necessity having it revisit, and there were definitely some people who just didn't want to acknowledge that the external issues that were going on around us we're going to have a pretty dramatic impact to the organization. I know it's one thing I found most challenging was to intrude or one really understood is a pared option it's a major atomic impact in us. It's going to affect us here locally and it did.

As the external environmental changes were increasing, CEO-H-2's perceptions of and feeling about the situations were that "Some of the things that were happening early on in this crisis were pretty shocking and the expectation was said early on that that was going to get worse before it gets better." CEO-H-2's emotional and cognitive responses to the internal and external events included:

So as a leader of the organization, of course my first thought is like I'm running the numbers through my head and I'm trying to get my arms around the size and the scope of the issue. It became clear to me early on that probably the most important issue that I needed to get in front of was how this news was going to impact the staff because they were reading about and seeing friends and neighbors losing jobs.

When contemplating if experiences over the last couple of years could be described as chaos, CEO-H-2 believed the experiences could be so described as:

Certainly externally, if you could use, although I hadn't used the term before, but you certainly could use the term 'chaotic' or 'chaos' when you look at what happened on Wall Street which the Dow Jones Industrial hit 14,000 in a relatively short amount of time that's down to 6,000. So that's certainly not a normal market that would border on a chaotic market. If you look at the actions of the US government in defense to that, trying to keep the economy from complete free fall, I think you could also say that was somewhat chaotic where the Congress said, "Well, we're going to spend $700 billion to buy these toxic assets and after that legislation passed and was enacted, they didn't spend any of that money on acquiring toxic assets. They instead recapitalize major financial players, so you could say that's chaotic.

When recalling if responses were as timely and/or creative as needed CEO-H-2 stated that:

I think in hindsight, I'm not going to second guess any of the decisions we made. I think they were timely. I think they were appropriate. I think they were in line with the situation at the time, so I would say, yes.

Individual descriptions: VP-H-1. VP-H-1 first noticed the external environmental changes that threatened the organization were:

I think one of the biggest things that we've seen was the high stability of IndyMac Bank that occurred in California that time period between IndyMac failing and when Lehman failed on September. It was really when we started taking notice and watching Bloomberg a whole lot closer, MSNBC, and listening the various experts and during that time all the data was negative no matter if we're talking about foreclosures. We're talking about home values, we're talking unemployment. That's really when we started looking within and trying to identify risk within our own organization around that time.

As the external danger signals increased, the first signs of internal dysfunction were:

I think the first sign was disagreements in management as far as what data meant first of all. And you have disagreements on what the data means, you have disagreements on how to move forward from there. Namely the corporate crisis, how serious is it. Is it is so serious that it can catch you up and you look other alternatives or are you in with everybody else to stand up? So I would say there was time period that there was deep divisions in management on what the data meant and how to move forward and that was-- those divisions are healed overtime but that was my foresight.

As the external environmental changes were increasing, VP-H-1's perceptions of and feeling about the situations were:

I think overall I think at the beginning of the-- I would have to say I was on the emotional kind of rollercoaster and experiencing a lot of different emotions. Just bringing in all the information and first of all I guess there was a period of a -- where I would not believe these events were unfolding then went to the I guess, movement to the area, I guess there's so much that's out of our control.

VP-H-1's emotional and cognitive responses to the internal and external events included "Every move that we made as a management team, was just big and as a management team was very calculated."

When contemplating if experiences over the last couple of years could be described as chaos, VP-H-1 believed the experiences could be described as "Chaos, on a daily basis, the amount of email updates or watching the new cycles, putting on Bloomberg, we're witnessing chaos on the daily basis." When recalling if responses were as timely and/or creative as needed. VP-H-1 stated:

> I'm a much better manager and I'm able to face... hopefully never face what we faced in the last couple of years again but better suited to face challenges in the future because of it. But I can't go back and second guess, those decisions have been made.

Individual descriptions: VP-H-2. VP-H-2 first noticed the external environmental changes that threatened the organization as follows:

> I would say in 2007 as we start to see the market values of -- in the mortgage backed security market deteriorate. And how would be when we realize what GAP accounting has -- the way GAP accounting has an effect on the balance sheet whenever those mortgage-backed security market values decline.

> They're impaired, but there have been no losses right now as the GAP accounting forces you to recognize those losses in a certain way through -- of a temporary impairment type charges and when it really set-in for me about how that affects a balance sheet, then it was a matter of trying to visualize. Well as a matter of watching things happen and visualizing how they're going to continue to ripple through and affect balance

sheets a world away from us and how that ripples back to us.

and the danger signals were:

> In 2007, we saw these things happening, and we personally didn't really understand the effect until I started seeing how GAP accounting was affecting balance sheets and causing liquidity problems, causing counterparty risk problems and how that ripples back down. You got your Lehman's and your Merrill's up here and you think that they're worlds away, they can never affect us. And then all of a sudden U.S. Corporate, well, that's a world away, it can never affect us and all of a sudden… these people are a lot closer to us than the original guys were and understanding that ripple effect.

As the external danger signals increased, the first signs of internal dysfunction were:

> When we went into a cost control mode. And I was actually very pleased with the reaction from staff of some of the in depth conversations about economics and interest rates, cycles and neo curves and stuff and how those affect you.

As the external environmental changes were increasing, VP-H-2's perceptions of, and feeling about the situations were "the internal situations where that this is deadly serious and this could take us down if we don't pay attention to it and we don't react in the right way." VP-H-2's emotional and cognitive responses to the internal and external events included "The initial emotion was the anger and disbelief, that sort of thing, but then, very quickly, my personality has always been not to focus on how something bad happened to me, but how do I deal with it going forward with." When contemplating if experiences over the last couple of years could be described as chaos, VP-H-2 believed that "I certainly think that the initial events up to the Lehman Brothers failure, and the passage of TARP could be described as chaotic." VP-H-2 stated that, "I wouldn't change any of the decisions we've made up to this point" when recalling if responses were as timely and/or creative as needed.

Individual descriptions: CEO-D-1. CEO-D-1 first noticed the external environmental changes that threatened the organization:

> I think the end of 2007, we started having members that came in, that were concerned about our balances, asking what type of investments that we were making, all those type of things, the safety and soundness of the credit union.

and the danger signals were:

> The stock market going way down, that was a sign. There was also the earnings of the corporates at the time, and there was -- they started having some significant losses for the first time. So all those things were kind of coming to -- there was a little bit of panic at the end of 2007, I think, that really started things, where there was some concern with the economy.

As the external danger signals increased, the first signs of internal dysfunction were "A little bit of delinquency with credit cards, those started going bad first." As the external environmental changes were increasing, CEO-D-1's perceptions of and feeling about the situations were "I think more frustration than anything is the way I would categorize it, because it has just been one thing after another, after another, this year." CEO-D-1's emotional and cognitive responses to the internal and external events included "Frustrating…what I did is went home and kicked the dog a lot. But really, as far as going forward, we just had to…not react too quickly."

When contemplating if experiences over the last couple of years could be described as chaos, CEO-D-1 believed the experiences could be described as follows: "Internally, from a credit union's perspective, I don't think there was chaos involved. I don't think there was any panic. There was concern I would say, more so, but it was…as far as the economy." When recalling if responses were as timely and/or creative as needed, CEO-D-1 stated:

> Well, it's always easy in hindsight to say, what would you have done better, what would you have done different? The best was we moved branch locations back when the economy was really good, so it would have cost us a lot more than what it would have been if we had waited another year.

Individual descriptions: CEO-D-2. CEO-D-2 first noticed the external environmental changes that threatened the organization "Mine is totally different. I mean, we came up a record year in 2008 and 2009 -- our plan was going great, record, record profits, record everything, and then to get slammed, I didn't see it coming." CEO-D-2 believed the danger signals were "the corporate crisis and NCUA stepping in, and like I say, it kind of blind sighted us." As the external danger signals increased, the first signs of internal dysfunction were "I think it was the increase in deposits in ours, which you say is a good, but...there was a point that it became a bad thing, because my capital was shrinking and my assets were increasing, and I think that was the first." As the external environmental changes were increasing, CEO-D-2's perceptions of and feeling about the situations were "It was kind of one of frustration. It was kind of one of disbelief, kind of shock, a lot of it was a shock. Like I said, we didn't see it coming." CEO-D-2's emotional and cognitive responses to the internal and external events included "I think my initial emotional response was disappointment, but I also saw that things changed for me. It gave me a different perspective, because I would go to my board and it would be anger and they wanted to blame someone."

When contemplating if experiences over the last couple of years could be described as chaos CEO-D-2 believed the experiences could be described as "I don't think I ever saw it as chaotic, as far as internally. Like I say, you just need to step up and do it." CEO-D-2 stated that "I don't know what I would have done different. Being a small credit union...we were limited in our choices and what we can do" when recalling if responses were as timely and/or creative as needed.

Individual descriptions: SM-D-1. SM-D-1 first noticed the external environmental changes that threatened the organization:

> I think I first noticed around the beginning of 2008. How did I notice? Well, of course there was a lot of stuff in the news. You started seeing some of these companies struggling, and getting bailouts and stuff. You started seeing a lot of the housing crisis. On a personal level, I was trying to sell my house right around that time, and there was nothing moving or anything like that. Over six months' time I think I got two people just even look at it and no offers. So those types of things are how I noticed.

SM-D-1 believed the danger signals were:

> It wasn't a ton, but we did have a certain amount of members that did start asking, what's going on, what are you guys seeing, what do you thing is going to happen? And I think, yeah, a lot of it was the money coming over, flight to safety, coming out of the stock market and stuff. So I think those were the biggest things we saw.

As the external environmental changes were increasing, SM-D-1's perceptions of and feeling about the situations were:

> My feelings were being upset, especially at the external factors, at just the way that things came down on that. As far as internal, I mean, I think our credit union has responded well and our people have handled it well, and accepted what's happening, and trying to do what we can to make sure that internally as an organization we are going to fight through it.

SM-D-1's emotional and cognitive responses to the internal and external events included:

I wouldn't say me, personally, that I was overemotional to any of it. I mean, I think when we sit down and look at what we need to do internally as a response to all this, I think we try to take emotion out of it, try to say, okay, what do we need to do to make sure that we survive this organization.

When contemplating if experiences over the last couple of years could be described as chaos, SM-D-1 said, "I don't know if I would use chaos as a word to describe the whole thing. Again, I mean if it continues and gets worse, then, yeah, we might see it. If you see more credit unions that are…I think credit unions as a whole have always been conservative and have been able to withstand what's happened." SM-D-1 stated that "I think we reacted well, because when we started seeing some of the signs, we started looking at other avenues, like the Federal Home Loan Bank and other commercial banks to maybe move some things over" when recalling if responses were as timely and/or creative as needed.

Individual descriptions: CEO-A-1. CEO-A-1 first noticed the external environmental changes that threatened the organization as follows:

We first noticed the early signs of the financial downturn. I guess we started hearing about the weaknesses in some of the securities markets and particularly specific to some of the early problems that were being experienced on the West Coast, trying to quantify that back to a year.

CEO-A-1 believed the danger signals were:

So it's probably different levels of that risk out there of the environmental decline and how it impacted us. We could see it but you didn't -- you could kind of relate it to your local environment and you could gain separation and a feeling for where you related, but then all of a sudden, there are other factors that came in. I don't think we really realized the impact of it on the corporate credit unions until all that came to light and we had a good realization of how that was going to impact us, which turned out to be the greatest impact of all.

As the external danger signals increased, the first signs of internal dysfunction were:

As we kind of went through the process, we started seeing more of the downturn externally and in external environments. I think internally, honestly we've seen some deterioration in loan performance and we noticed that early on. We started to see more underemployment, unemployment, those two factors coming into play. Within our organization though, we've seen some slowing loan demand. We saw an influx in savings, traditional things which you would see in this type of a market. They haven't necessarily had an adverse effect on our overall performance but it was more manifested in the way our members, consumer members, the way they went about conducting their business.

As the external environmental changes were increasing, CEO-A-1's perceptions of and feeling about the situations were:

So I think just dealing with that and managing that process, why you do see it this industry-wide and it does impact everybody. There is a lot of frustration. There's a degree of frustration of not being able to achieve your own individual goals that you have to manage, manipulate and change your own strategic objectives specific to a lot of this stuff. So probably internally for us, it's been more of a -- we continue to make good profitability. We have continued to maintain good operations to be able to provide services, do everything we want to do. It's maybe just the frustration level of having to adjust our overall growth, our strategic objectives, expectations to the environment a little bit more than we have in the past.

CEO-A-1's emotional and cognitive responses to the internal and external events included:

> I would just kind of reiterate what I said, the answer to the last question here a little bit. I think it's a similar response of frustration with the process like when we first became aware of the situation. It took a long time and I'm not sure at this point we've ever been really given good indication about the regulators on -- I think we get inklings of information but never a good picture of what the real implications are. You almost -- you're left kind of wondering if they really know or if they have -- how well defined their perspective is. So it just adds to that frustration in what's going on there. So I think a lot of our frustration has manifested itself in the regulatory environment and the way they -- not necessarily dealt with but the way they communicated it across us. So I think that's been the biggest issue.

When contemplating if experiences over the last couple of years could be described as chaos, CEO-A-1 commented, "No, I don't believe I would. I think the way the situation, the economic situation has manifested itself in our environment, in our local environment hasn't been chaotic, nor did we ever perceive it to be." CEO-A-1 stated that "I think our responses...looking back over, I can't see where I would've responded or felt that we could have or should have or potentially should've considered responding any differently" when recalling if responses were as timely and/or creative as needed.

Individual descriptions: CEO-A-2. CEO-A-2 first noticed the external environmental changes that threatened the organization "When and how I started hearing about it is just on national media, what was happening outside of Texas, and then it came closer to home." CEO-A-2 believed the danger signals were "when we heard the NCUA announced and then we heard the corporate capitalization, we knew then that we had felt trust and prior to that, that was going to be on uneven ground and it could directly impact us by the loss of our membership shares and the assessment and the stabilization." As the external danger signals increased, the first signs of internal dysfunction were that:

> We saw a great influx of deposits. Our loans slowed, so in response, we started a new loan program which was a little bit too successful, FirstLine Mortgage, internally home equity, FirstLine Mortgage, so we put a lot of loans extremely successfully at low rates so we had an interest rate risk that we had had before, but we had to do something with that money.

As the external environmental changes were increasing, CEO-A-2's perceptions of and feeling about the situations were that "there's a negative feeling that we are having to now swallow something that we did not directly create. At the same time, it's part of business." CEO-A-2's emotional and cognitive responses to the internal and external events included a "frustration of feeling like the regulator did not handle it in a thoughtful manner. Maybe it was knee-jerk initially when the response could've been more well-thought out or timed even now with the conservatorship, that kind a blindside decision."

When contemplating if experiences over the last couple of years could be described as chaos, CEO-A-2 believed the experiences could be described as "I don't believe it has affected us here in Texas in a chaotic manner. I think some of the decisions may have not been well thought out, but chaotic is not a word I would use." CEO-A-2 stated that "I guess on hindsight, you could have accrued for assessments. Creative, I don't know. I'm not a creative person, so it would be hard for me to think of how creatively it would've changed what happened" when recalling if responses were as timely and/or creative as needed.

Individual descriptions: CEO-A-3. CEO-A-3 first noticed the external environmental changes that threatened the organization:

> I recognized them pretty early because I'm a former credit union examiner and I have a strong background in the investment area. I have an undergraduate in

71

Economics and an MBA with a dual concentration in Finance as well as Investment Management, and I used to review the top 100 investment portfolios, state-chartered credit unions as far as their safety and soundness when I was an examiner. And I saw that the levels of risk-taking had escalated pretty dramatically. The quality of the securities had really fallen quite a bit and I didn't really think that the regulators were doing a whole lot about it.

CEO-A-3 believed the danger signals were:

I recognized it pretty early. But there's not a lot you can do other than try to back down the hatchet a little bit, understand that that's the first and foremost priority, is the maintenance of a safe and sound condition, and making sure that you haven't taken excessive risks that can impact your organization and impact your member's viewpoint of the organization.

As the external danger signals increased, the first signs of internal dysfunction were that:

I'm having a little hard time understanding internal dysfunction. I think of it more as internal disruption probably. I don't know that we have the dysfunction so much as it groups outside of our credit union that had the dysfunction from underwriting and core securities and other things.

As the external environmental changes were increasing, CEO-A-3's perceptions of and feeling about the situations confronted were:

Pissed off. I also feel that we have a share insurer that's totally unaccountable to credit unions and we have no voice or ability to influence that organization other than through a very widely... express our opinions through them getting comment letters, our state-chartered regulator.

CEO-A-3's emotional and cognitive responses to the internal and external events included that "I wasn't pleased to what was indicated but after your annoyance, frustration, it sort of passes."

When contemplating if experiences over the last couple of years could be described as chaos, CEO-A-3 believed the experiences could be described as:

> We didn't have chaos but I think if you look at things nationwide, there was chaos in a lot of different parts of the country. We were more insulated as CEO-A-1 and CEO-A-2 had said here in Texas. So it did impact us probably to a chaotic level but I think it was a chaotic event. We just didn't have quite some of the repercussions that some of the others did. But some other states like California and Nevada, Arizona, states like that, Utah, have some pretty significant impacts from this. And our view is it's chaotic in the sense that it's going to impact us for 10 years. So it didn't really create chaos for us but I do view it as a chaotic event.

CEO-A-3 stated that, "I can't really think of a lot that I would do differently. I mean, there are situations like that. You just try to have the best response as you can. And I also think you want to try to operate as normally as possible" when recalling if responses were as timely and/or creative as needed.

Individual descriptions: CEO-H-3. CEO-H-3 first noticed the external environmental changes that threatened the organization:

> When you start getting vehicles back that you don't normally repossess, we live in Texas, and we didn't used to repo a lot of trucks and then people retain the vehicles. They handle their business here. When you start seeing anomalies like that start happening in your portfolio, it's a pretty good indicator that things are not

right out there in the market. When you start seeing long-term members have issues, and even though they may have retained their jobs, it's a pretty telltale sign that something impactual has affected the economy, which has in essence affected the member.

CEO-H-3 believed the danger signals were that "When you start seeing long-term members have issues, and even though they may have retained their jobs, it's a pretty telltale sign that something impactful has affected the economy, which has in essence affected the member." As the external danger signals increased, the first signs of internal dysfunction were that:

In our leadership group, the first signals were, we were as a group being required to address more and more and more issues on a more frequent basis. Our weekly management team meetings became, not necessarily crisis, but they were more of kind of mini interventions. Instead of looking long-term, we were addressing short-term issues all the time. And that was probably my first major indicator that we could feel the dynamics changing in the credit union. We used to write two, three, five year plans, and now our management team is addressing -- our management meeting is addressing kind of current pending issues as they happen.

As the external environmental changes were increasing, CEO-H-3's perceptions of and feeling about the situations were "Well, to be blunt, I don't like it, but it's the world we have created. I feel like we live in the greatest country in the world, however, it's kind of, we have made our own mess, and it has got to be dealt with." CEO-H-3's emotional and cognitive responses to the internal and external events included "…as a matter of fact, probably the worst thing you can do is get your personal feelings caught up in it, whether you agree with it or don't agree with it."

When contemplating if experiences over the last couple of years could be described as chaos, CEO-H-3 believed the experiences could be described as:

No, I don't believe I would use the term chaos. I feel --
no, I would definitely not use chaos. Over my 21 years
of experience, I think that as a manager I have done a
really good job of addressing issues as they come, and I
think the experience of having dealt with those issues is
kind -- it kind of makes the manager that you are today.
The one thing or the one dynamic that has changed is I
think we are making more decisions on a quicker basis
now. I guess when we weren't in an essence crisis, you
may make one to ten decisions in a month that were
pretty impactual on the credit union, I kind of feel like
we are making one to ten on a weekly basis at this point.

CEO-H-3 stated that:

I think as a leader we, and in our organization, we
have been timely and responsive. I think just in the
industry that we work in, there has been a whole lot of
them that have gone by the wayside, and I think almost
anybody who is left at this point has had to be timely
and responsive and still be in good shape. It's not as easy
as it used to be

when recalling if responses were as timely and/or creative as needed.

Individual descriptions: VP-H-3. VP-H-3 first noticed the external
environmental changes that threatened the organization "Collections
related activities, I think we have noticed external changes impact
the credit union when regulations or the regulatory environment has
changed, which happened early this year, and we knew some changes
were coming down the pipe through the midyear." VP-H-3 believed the
danger signals were that "the external environment change or regulation
change actually impact us." As the external danger signals increased,
the first signs of internal dysfunction were that:

The most impact usually is at the front line or the
bottom line of the credit union's income. Even though
we are not for profit, we still have to maintain our

income to a significant level so that we can maintain our capital ratio.

As the external environmental changes were increasing, VP-H-3's perceptions of and feeling about the situations were "Even though if we don't like it, we have to deal with it." VP-H-3's emotional and cognitive responses to the internal and external events included:

Emotionally or personally, even if I don't like it, as leaders we have to get our emotion out of the equations when we deal with other people or our followers, or the employees, or the staff members that we have.

When contemplating if experiences over the last couple of years could be described as chaos, VP-H-3 believed the experiences could be described as "I would also say no. I don't think I would describe anything with chaos per se, even though there are sometimes that we may experience some dysfunction within the leadership team or within the organization." VP-H-3 stated that, "I would say yes; if I hadn't had the timely or creative responses then I wouldn't be here at the organization" when recalling if responses were as timely and/or creative as needed.

Meaning Units

The Moustakas analytical procedure allowed for the identification of meaning units within the transcripts by eliminating similar responses, in favor of non-repetitive and non-overlapping statements of the participant's experiences. Developing meaning from the interviews helps to develop an understanding of participant's lived experiences and to make a connection by identifying a synergy of the recalled experiences and meanings of participants (Moustakas, 1994; Walker, 2007). This section presents examples of meaning units derived from the transcripts of the interviews.

Question 1. When and how did you first notice the external environmental changes that threatened your organization? What were the danger signals? The meaning units derived from responses to this question included rapid interest rate decline and increase in delinquencies. Other meaning units included rapid bank and credit union failures, negative local and national media reports, decreases in loan quality, and fast-paced operational changes.

Question 2. *As the external danger signals increased, what were the first signals of internal dysfunction?* The meaning units derived from responses to this question included leadership disagreement on how to react to the financial crisis, finding common ground on reaction strategies, ability to understand what was occurring within the financial markets, loan quality issues, pressure on capital, and worried about safety and soundness.

Question 3. *How would you describe your perceptions of and feelings about the external and internal situations you found yourself confronted with?* The meaning units included anger, wanting to hold someone accountable, shocked, frustrated, aggressive response, apprehension, and trying to find a new normal.

Question 4. *How would you describe your emotional and cognitive responses to the external and internal events you were required to deal with?* The meaning units included the needs to remove emotions from decision-making, to contain anger, to focus on the job, and to reduce rumors by increased honest internal and external communication. Other meaning units include taking a proactive approach, denial instead of developing strategies, not reacting quickly enough, and a sense of annoyance in having to deal with a problem that someone else created.

Question 5. *If you have not already done so, would you use the word chaos to describe any aspect of your experiences over the past two years?* Yes, chaos would be a correct word to describe the experiences over the last two years. Other meaning units included identifying that a major operational paradigm shift was occurring, experiencing external chaos, and experiencing limited internal chaos.

Question 6. *Using hindsight, were your responses as timely and/ or creative as needed?* The meaning units from question six included leaders' not wanting to second-guess the decision-making processes that occurred within the organization and leaders feeling forced to recognize alternative decisions because the financial situation was changing rapidly.

Common Themes

Identification of the most common, dominant, significant lived experiences of the participants resulted in common themes (Moustakas, 1994). Common themes reduce the large amounts of data into a manageable collection of patterned participant experience. The common themes in this research study was isolated and identified after meaning units, as presented above, were reduced further. The common themes included the fast-paced changes to the overall internal and external operating environment, leadership disagreement on internal and external data analysis, anger, shock, frustration, and surprised by the aggressive response needed, the need to reduce rumors and fear, external environment seemed chaotic, and the crisis forced creativity.

Theme 1. Question 1 was, *When and how did you first notice the external environmental changes that threatened your organization? What were the danger signals?* The common themes included rapid decline of the economy, the fast-paced changes to the regulations and to the overall internal and external financial environment, and the rapid failures of banks, corporate credit unions, and regular credit union failures. Comments included "pricing of mortgaged back securities and how those prices at the bottom of the market fell," "Wachovia Bank and Washington Mutual get merged into mega banks in a matter of days," and "started hearing about the weaknesses in some of the securities markets." Other common themes included the rapid rise in mortgage delinquencies, the speed in which the economy was entering a recession, and overall safety and soundness of the financial industry.

Theme 2. Question 2 was, *As the external danger signals increased, what were the first signs of internal dysfunction?* The common themes included leadership disagreement on internal and external data analysis, pressure placed on earnings, and leaders required to deal with more short-term issues, which required rapid problem solving. Comments included "deterioration in loan performance," "there was time period that there was deep divisions in management on what the data meant and how to move forward," and "when we went into a cost control mode." Other common themes included the panic with major Wall Street firms, investment companies, and consumers, the frustration on how to how leaders should lead through the crisis, and trying to identify the overall impact of how external changes in the operating environment were going to influence the organization.

Theme 3. Question 3 was, *How would you describe your perceptions of and feelings about the external and internal situations you found yourself confronted with?* The common themes included anger, shock, frustration, and being surprised by the aggressive response needed. Comments included "the initial emotion was the anger and disbelief," "capital was shrinking and my assets were increasing," and "there's a degree of frustration of not being able to achieve your own individual goals." Other common themes included not to overreact to the crisis, knowing that the situation could get worst before getting better, how to lead through the crisis, and an overall feeling of not being in control of the situation.

Theme 4. Question 4 was, *How would you describe your emotional and cognitive responses to the external and internal events you were required to deal with?* A common theme was the need to reduce rumors and fear. Other themes include that the need for problem solving increased dramatically and a general sense of annoyance that leaders had to deal with a problem someone else caused. Comments included "frustration with the process like when we first became aware of the situation," "frustration of feeling like the regulator did not handle it in a thoughtful manner," and "well, to be blunt, I don't like it, but it's the world we have created."

Theme 5. Question 5 was, *If you have not already done so, would you use the word chaos to describe any aspect of your experiences over the past two years?* The common theme was that the external environment seemed chaotic. Comments included "chaos from a perspective of very little control over the situation," "certainly externally, if you could use, although I hadn't used the term before, but you certainly could use the term 'chaotic' or 'chaos' when you look at what happened on Wall Street," and "chaos, on a daily basis."

Theme 6. Question 6 was, *Using hindsight, were your responses as timely and/or creative as needed?* The common theme was that the crisis forced creativity. Comments included "I would say yes; if I hadn't had the timely or creative responses then I wouldn't be here at the organization," "I think almost anybody who is left at this point has had to be timely and responsive," and "just try to have the best response as you can."

Summary

Chapter 4 described the findings obtained from the systemic analysis of the data collected from 12 interviews using purposive sampling to examine the experiences, perceptions, attitudes, and behaviors of credit union leaders in charge of individual credit unions during a period of economic crisis and contraction by exploring meanings and themes of lived experiences. The objective of using a purposive sample is to find the best informants possible with which to identify the phenomena, themes, and within the themes the patterns of experience (Denzin & Lincoln, 2005).

Participants responded to open-ended questions that allowed participants to communicate their responses to the problem under investigation and to explore emergent themes during the research (Creswell, 2005; Moustakas, 1994). The general purpose of qualitative inquiry is to explore, describe, and explain phenomenon (Marshall & Rossman, 2006). The phenomenological data analysis process allowed participants to be reflective, by establishing the context of participants' experiences and constructing the meaning of those experiences (Flood, 2010).

Chapter 4 provided an overview of the research interviews, analytical process procedures, highlights from the raw data, identification of meaning units, and identification of themes that further synthesized the large amounts of collected research data from the four interviews. Chapter 5 presents an interpretation of these findings in the form of a composite description of the participant's experiences along with potential implications, recommendations for future action, and suggestions for future research.

Chapter 5
CONCLUSIONS AND RECOMMENDATIONS

The general problem, creating the need for the research, was that the financial crisis of 2008 and ensuing recession created turmoil within the entire financial industry. The turmoil included pressure on deposit insurance funds, monetary market operations, financial institution solvency concerns, liquidity and credit anxiety, and blurred regulatory boundaries (Goodhart, 2008). The turmoil within the financial industry has caused and is causing financial institutions of different types to experience organizational stress, resulting in poor risk management, increased internal conflict, lost opportunity, and defensive management instead of producing creative leadership (Shiller, 2008). Economic contraction has forced leaders to develop strategies that focus on survival rather than on performance (Shore, 2009). The current recession has caused credit union leaders to tightened budgets, experience decreased revenue, decreased employee compensation, to defer branch expansion, close branch offices, and has caused interpersonal and interdepartmental organizational chaos (Gustafson, 2009). The purpose of this exploratory qualitative phenomenological research was to explore the experiences, perceptions, attitudes, and behaviors of 12 credit union leaders in charge of individual credit unions during a period of economic contraction. The qualitative method selected was considered appropriate for the research because a qualitative method is exploratory and seeks thematic rather than numerical data (Creswell, 2005). The phenomenological design was considered appropriate because the investigation was focused on the subjective experience of the credit union leaders.

Chapter 1 introduced the background of the financial crisis, specified the problem and the purpose of the proposed research, its conceptual framework, and the academic and social significance of the research. Chapter 2 reviewed the literature on the history of credit unions, credit union leadership practices, the current financial crisis, and identified gaps in the literature about credit union leadership. The review of the literature included recent attempts to use concepts and models from chaos and systems theory in the explanation of leadership behavior in organizations under extreme stress. Chapter 3 presented the method used to conduct this research and provided details relevant to the research design, the population selected and sampled, along with issues of confidentiality and informed consent. Chapter 4 provided an overview of the research interviews, analytical procedures, highlights from the raw data, identification of meaning units, and identification of emergent themes from the interviews. Chapter 5 provides an interpretation of the interview data following phenomenological reduction and the construction of a composite description of the credit union leader experience of the crisis of 2008. The chapter concludes with a discussion of the potential implications of the findings, recommendations for future action by the leaders of credit unions, and suggestions for future research.

Research Procedures

The analytical process used for this research was adapted from the mode of data analysis developed by Moustakas (1994). Following Moustakas, the data analysis took place in six steps. These steps included transcripts of the statements made during each interview were read and reread, the statements, phrases, or words that seemed to be descriptors of a subjectively significant aspect of relevant experience were coded and highlighted followed by the construction of lists of the highlighted descriptors, and the development of *meaning units* of the participant's experience. The remaining steps included clustering the related and invariant (recurring) meaning units into *themes* and the meaning units and themes obtained from each participant were used to construct an *individual description* of the experience in question for each participant, using verbatim quotations as examples. The final step in this analytical process was the construction of a single composite narrative of the experience derived from the 12 individual descriptions of the experience that is, a generalized description of the meanings and essences of the experience, representing the experience of the group as a whole.

Developing meaning from the interviews helps to develop an understanding of participants' lived experiences and to make a connection by identifying a synergy of the recalled experiences and meanings of participants (Moustakas, 1994; Walker, 2007). The meaning units were further analyzed to identify themes. Themes allow for the identification of the most common, dominant, significant lived experiences of the participants (Moustakas, 1994). Themes reduce the large amounts of data into a collection of participants' experiences by conducting a detailed analysis of the data (Creswell, 2005) and further synthesize the data to identify leadership behavior and reaction to significant internal and external changes to the operating environment.

From Findings to Interpretation: The Composite Description

Step 6 of the analysis allowed for the composite descriptions of the participant (Moustakas, 1994). After an intensive examination of the meaning units, themes, and individual descriptions, a composite description of the participant was constructed. A composite narrative of the experience from the 12 individual descriptions of the experience is a generalized description of the meanings and essences of the experience, representing the experience of the group as a whole.

Changing operating environment. The inquiry into sensitivity to initial conditions that produce different outcomes led to the belief that disruptions could alter the direction of future events (Sun & Scott, 2005). Uncertainties, unpredictability, and nonlinear dynamics could occur within systems (Stapleton, Hanna, & Ross, 2006). These uncertainties, unpredictability, and nonlinear dynamics can cause chaos within any system that is susceptible to variations of disorder caused by internal or external environmental changes (Ng, 2009). Chaotic events are temporary changes occurring in complex systems that create uncertainty and was theorized by Lorenz (Kim, Payne, & Tan, 2006; Yolles, 2007). Lorenz (1963), a pioneer of chaos theory, popularized the "butterfly effect" which, for many, is the hallmark of chaos theory. The concept called attention to physical and social systems of having "dependency or sensitivity to initial conditions" (Perla & Carifio, 2005, p. 269) and systems theory.

Developed more than 40 years ago by Ludwig von Bertalanffy, systems theory may serve as an alternative to existing organizational theories that focus on isolated unidirectional organizational relations (Kramer, 2007). Von Bertalanffy argued that organizations are open systems that have certain universal characteristics. These characteristics include hierarchical structures, the use of energy from external environments to support sustainability, being partially bound by internal and external exchanges, self-regulations, and the capacity of reaching a final state of operations by changes based on emerging conditions (Davidson & Rowe, 2009).

The participants generally first noticed the external environmental changes that threatened the organization when the rate of financial institutions failing increased, especially when some well known financial institutions failed, rapid decreased value of mortgage backed securities, rapid decline of the stock market, rapid government intervention in the financial market, and media reports of instability in the financial market. The danger signals that began to or could have influenced participants' organizations included bank failures, an increase in unemployment, and financial market panic. As the danger signals increased, the first signs of internal organizational dysfunction included the speed at which the regulatory environment was changing, decreased organizational profitability, management team required to deal with more issues, increased deposits and a decrease in loan demand, and decrease in loan quality that caused an increase in loan delinquencies.

Leadership emotional reaction. Chaos in an organization creates many challenges for leaders. The main challenge is the ability to manage followers. People tend to follow blindly, even if their conformity leads in the wrong direction (Clegg, Kornberger, & Pitsis, 2005). Chaos can create opportunities for leaders to lead in the wrong direction, with followers closely behind. To find clarity in such an unclear environment, leaders should be able to recognize whether the chaos is truly chaos or merely organizational complexity.

Prigogine (1984) argued that systems theory could explain how chaotic events influence deterministic nonlinear systems within the organization (Svensson, Wood, & Mathisen, 2008). Prigogine believed that when internal or external events occur within an organization, the potential for unpredictable behavior increases (Svensson, 2009). The transition from old norms to new norms can strain an organization. The moment at which leaders within the organization choose which path could most influence organizational sustainability is called a bifurcation point. A bifurcation point consists of divergent, abrupt, and discontinuous changes in the system that forces leaders to choose an organizational direction that can increase organizational sustainability (Zhong & Low, 2009). When faced with making a decision at the bifurcation point, leaders could face the possibility that their organization may respond in one of five different ways. The old norms may dominate and systems may retreat to a previous state, or, newly emerging systems may dominate and the systems could begin to stabilize, or systems may compete for equal attention, create tension, and oscillate between new and old (Svensson, Wood, & Mathisen, 2008). The systems may create additional bifurcation points and generate confusion, until the systems settle, or finally, the systems could never settle, creating a continuous loop of unstable patterns (Svensson, Wood, & Mathisen, 2008).

The participants described their perceptions of and feelings about the external and internal situations they found themselves confronted with as anger, wanting accountability, shock, frustration, and disbelief. The emotional and cognitive responses to the external and internal events the participants were required to deal with included annoyance, frustration, having to keep personal feelings out of decision-making, and disappointment of having to deal with a situation that they were not involved in causing.

Chaos and decision-making. Chaos within an organization has a way of appearing quickly and without warning. The environment organizations perform in is becoming more complex, and leaders are becoming entrenched in the day-to-day pressures of the organization (Mason, 2007). Leaders should become more aware of the order and disorder found within their organizations, rather than being surprised by sudden chaos (Mason, 2007).

Leaders can employ chaos theory as a sensitizing model for improving decision-making (Samli, 2006). During periods of organizational chaos, leaders often need to process a large amount of information about the internal and external operating environment. Today, much of the information about internal and external operating environment tends to originate from changing technology, global competition, the power structure of the organization, and the changing lifestyles of consumers. The information leaders may need to process can include many of these items, or only a few, but either way, leaders may benefit from the successful processing of information during chaotic events.

The attempt to apply chaos theory to an analysis of organizational management has some management philosophers encouraging leaders to recognize the importance of remaining responsive to the ever-changing demands of internal and external environments (Bums, 2002). Introducing chaos theory into organizational leadership has become a new approach to leadership psychology and philosophy, promising to transform leadership and management theories (Bums, 2002).

Participants described the experiences over the past two years as controlled chaos, chaotic, external chaos but not internal chaos, and a situation that was not necessarily chaotic but could have become chaotic if they had not taken action. Participants believed that their responses were creative and timely as needed, trying to do their best considering the circumstances and the rapid pace of change, and not wanting to second-guess their decisions.

Implications for Leadership

The implications of the research for credit union leaders and leadership studies may help leaders understanding how to respond to organizational crises signaled by negative changes in the general environment within which they operate. The decisions made by leaders in response to small signals can influence various internal organizational variables. Leaders' decision-making processes can have far-reaching organizational sustainability implications (McKenzie, Woolf, van Winkelen, & Morgan, 2009).

Credit union leaders. The research and analysis, based in chaos theory, provides credit union leaders with a broader perspective, which may provide helpful for increasing how leaders respond to organizational crises caused by negative changes in the general environment. The common themes identified include:

1. Disruptions in the general operating environment can result in fast-paced changes.
2. Leadership disagreement on internal and external data analysis.
3. Leaders felt anger, shock, frustration, and surprised by the aggressive response needed.
4. Leaders reported a need to reduce rumors and fear among stakeholders.
5. The need for problem solving increased dramatically while leaders were feeling general sense of annoyance of having to deal with disruptions.
6. Participants felt that a crisis forced creative leadership decisions.

As credit unions have grown in size and complexity, their vulnerability to external environmental changes has also increased. Government laws and general economic conditions is the major source of organizational and operational change for credit unions (Barron & Hannan, 1994). During the recent periods of credit union growth, credit union leaders were guided by the simplistic behavioral idea that to increase employee motivation, leaders simply needed to implement, or increase the use of, monetary incentive programs (Siemsen, Roth, & Balasubramanian, 2008). Any such simple behavioral assumption has the potential to impede credit union leadership behavior and decision-making during periods of unexpected change, similar to the financial crisis of 2008 (Basu, Raj, & Tchalian, 2008).

Credit union leadership practices seem to reflect ideas from many different leadership theories. These leadership theories include path-goal, transactional, transformational, leader-member exchange, situational, and servant. While leaders within the credit union industry often build leader and follower relationships based on a shared vision (Centini, 2005), the most common leadership practice used by credit union leaders is transformational (Colbert, Kristof-Brown, & Barrick, 2006). The findings of the research study may strengthen the use of transformational leadership practices among credit union leaders. Transformational leadership practices can increase leaders' recognition of changes to the operating environment, understanding the implications of emotional reactions by leaders to change, and the influences of chaos on the decision-making abilities of leaders (Colbert, Kristof-Brown, & Barrick, 2006).

Leadership Studies. Although theoretical knowledge exists in the literature about the application of chaos theory and general systems theory as models that seek to map disruptions that challenge normal events (Arciszewski, Sauer, & Schum, 2003), no practical applications of chaos theory relating to credit union leadership practices could be found. The findings of the current study represent new findings, specifically that disruptions in the internal and external operating environment can cause disagreement on internal and external data analysis of the disruption, rapid leadership problem solving, the operating environment can seem chaotic, and disruptions can force leadership decision-making creativity.

The field of leadership studies is changing with the development of new specialties within the many academic disciplines that touch on issues of leadership. With growing interest in general systems theory, cybernetics, and chaos theory, social scientists are unsure of how chaos theory can contribute, if at all, to a viable leadership theory. An increasing number of social scientists are experimenting with nonlinear concepts (Wheatley, 2006), which is behavior that is often unexpected, unpredictable, random behavior, despite leaders performing in a stable environment (Mendenhall, Macomber, & Cutright, 2000). As organizational challenges occur, the challenge of nonlinear behavior could most likely continue into the future, until corrected. Wheatley (2006) states, "The science of the seventeenth century cannot explain what we are challenged by in the twenty-first century" (p. 161).

The research may make an original contribution to leadership studies by continuing the effort to apply the perspectives of general systems and chaos theory to an understanding of leadership behavior in times of crisis. Chaos theory may also offer a potentially new perspective on a leader's capacity to change his or her approach, based on the needs of the organization, when experiencing what appear to be chaotic events. This adaptability may prove to be the most effective leadership skill a leader can display (Higgs & Rowland, 2005). The findings of this research study may allow credit union leaders use new models that recognize external changes that influence the sustainability of the organization.

Introducing general systems and chaos theory into organizational leadership has become a new approach to leadership psychology and philosophy, promising to influence leadership and management theories

(Bums, 2002). The significance of chaos theory for leadership studies lies in its heuristic power. If the challenges to normal events are observed through the lens of chaos theory, organizational leaders may make better-informed decisions in times of uncertainty.

Recommendations for Action: Two Models

Step 4 of the analysis allowed for the discovery of recurrent themes in the interview data through the identification of the most common, dominant, significant lived experiences of the participants (Moustakas, 1994). These themes included rapid decline of the economy the fast-paced changes to the regulations and overall internal and external financial environment; leaders' disagreement on internal and external data analysis; anger, shock, frustration, and surprise about the aggressive response needed; a need for problem solving; a seemingly chaotic external environment seemed chaotic; and crisis-driven creativity. The findings of the research study suggest two models that may help credit union leaders increase their capacities to change, based on the needs of the organization, when experiencing what appears to be the onset of chaotic events.

The first model is the organizational operation model represented in Figure 1. The second model is the degrees of freedom model represented in Figure 2. These two models were constructed by the author based on the findings of this research project. These two models support the identified common themes to help leaders identify and react to a rapid decline within the internal and external operating environments, identifying and resolving potential disagreements on internal and external data analysis, how shock, anger, frustration, and surprise can influence leadership capabilities, the need for problem solving, and the importance of creativity during crisis-driven events. To further support the common themes identified in this research project, existing leadership theories are integrated into these models. These theories include transformational by uniting followers and change followers' goals and beliefs, to represent a future vision, (Beugré, Acar, & Braun, 2006), systems theory helps leaders understand how thinking influences organizational mechanics, learning management, and organizational sustainability (Putnik, 2009), and situational leadership theory creates an environment that focuses on task behaviors by focusing on follower performance (Hughes, Ginnett, & Curphy, 2002).

Figure 1. Organizational Operation Model.

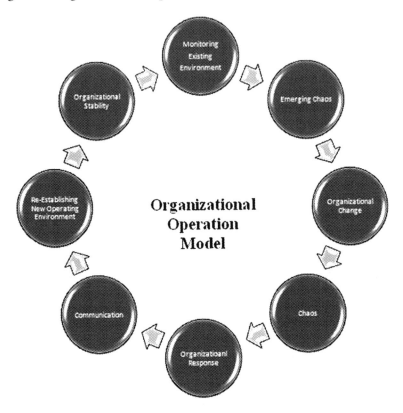

Organizational operation model. Based on the themes identified from the research study, the organizational operation model may help credit union leaders recognize the different stages the organization experiences when internal or external changes occur in the operating environment. The organizational operation model has eight stages. The first four stages include the monitoring of the existing environment, identifying an emerging chaotic environment, the amount of organizational change to respond to the chaotic environment, and recognizing the organization is in chaos. The remaining four stages include developing the organizational response to chaos, communicating the response to chaos to internal and external stakeholders, re-establishing a new operating norm, and establishing organizational stability. Once the organization has successfully navigated through the eight stages of the organizational operation model, leaders should begin again to operate at the monitoring existing environment stage.

The monitoring existing environment stage is where organizational leaders can monitor internal and external trends by identifying increases or decreases in those trends. Leaders may benefit from monitoring internal and external trends quarterly. These internal and external trends can include return on assets, capital, loan quality, investment quality, or financial market conditions. As suggested in the current study, leaders can monitor the environment through strategic and organizational intelligence. Participants indicated that as changes occurred in the existing environment, they became angry, wanted accountability and experienced shocked, frustration, and disbelief. Leaders can increase strategic and organizational intelligence through the organizational operational model, they can help make sense of their perceptions of, and feelings about, the external and internal situations they find themselves confronted with.

Prior to an organization's entering chaos, organizational leaders recognize that significant changes within the internal and external environment are occurring. These organizational changes may require some type of response, which can include leaders having to re-visit an existing strategic plan, to create new strategies, or to require action on behalf of leaders. Recognition of the leader's role in strategy development is important in order to help leaders re-visit the existing strategic plan, create new strategies, or require action on behalf of leaders. Credit union leaders can influence strategy development by encouraging senior management to think strategically and by involving multiple layers of employees to identify internal and external organizational strengths and weaknesses.

As organizational leaders re-visit the existing strategic plan or create new strategies, the period of chaos can create internal dysfunction. The internal dysfunction can be caused by leaders' disagreeing on internal and external data analysis and requiring leaders to deal with short-term issues that require rapid problem solving. In such instances, the leaders carry the potential of not solving the right problem. The organizational change stage and chaos stage can be emotional experiences for leaders leading to feelings of anger, shock, and frustration. If leaders are not prepared, they could be surprised by the aggressive responses needed. Leaders' solving problems successfully might increase movement of the organization though the chaos stage. The more prepared a leader is prior to the organizational change stage, the less dysfunction the organization may experience.

The organizational response stage occurs when organizational leaders begin the process of emerging from chaos and implementing changes to existing strategies or implementing new strategies. The pace at which organizational leaders implement organizational change during crisis increases by forcing leaders to respond rapidly to changes in the shifting operating environment. The speed at which an organization can respond is based on the capabilities of the internal and external stakeholders to adapt to change. This identification of current internal stakeholders' contributions to the organization can allow leaders to predict the success of organizational response. Identifying customers' ability to adapt to change is just as important because customers are sensitive to change may slow the organization's ability to emerge out of chaos. Communicating the need for change to internal and external stakeholders can increase the speed at which an organization transitions to the new operating environment stage.

The re-establishing new environment stage occurs when the organization begins to emerge from chaos and begins to identify a new operating norm. In this stage, organizational leaders can reflect on their experiences with the monitoring existing environment, emerging chaos, organizational change, chaos, organizational response, and communication stages to identify if responses were as timely and/or creative as needed. In the re-establishing new operating environment stage, the organization could still experience chaos if the right problems were not solved during the organizational change stage.

In the organizational stability stage, leaders have successfully navigated through internal or external environmental changes that created chaos. During this stage, leaders can benefit from re-evaluating their strategic and organizational perceptions. Once leaders have re-evaluated their perceptions and made necessary changes to strengthen how they monitor the internal and external environment, the organization transitions back to the monitoring existing environment stage and remains there until significant internal or external changes threaten the organization again.

Leadership practices that may assist leaders strengthen leader and follower relationships when transitioning through each of the eight stages could include transformational leadership theory. Transformational leaders, as described by Burns (1978), motivate followers to commit to a higher goal that is not based on their self-interest. Followers have traditionally classified transformational leaders as charismatic, inspirational, capable of stimulating others intellectually, and capable of individualized concern for others (Defee, Esper, & Mollenkopf, 2009). The effectiveness of transformational leaders is a consequence of their ability to unite followers and change followers' goals and beliefs, to represent a future vision for followers, and to motivate subordinates to perform beyond expectations (Beugré, Acar, & Braun, 2006).

Systems theory may help increase the understanding of the potential practical application of the organizational operational model. Systems theory is widely used within organizations to help understand organizational complexity. The use of systems theory helps leaders appreciate how chaordic systems thinking influences organizational mechanics, learning management, and organizational sustainability (Putnik, 2009). Hock, former CEO of Visa, developed chaordic system thinking in 1993 as a way to describe organizational environments that are both chaotic and ordered (Hock, 1999). Chaordic systems is defined as systems that allow leaders to have an increased level of consciousness, connectivity, dissipation, indeterminacy, and emergence that assists with achieving organizational sustainability (Putnik, 2009). Leaderships' ability to self-organization and being adaptive promotes internal and external cooperation and competition (Hock, 1999). Chaordic systems thinking consist of five characteristics, which include consciousness, connectivity, indeterminacy, dissipation, and emergence (Putnik, 2009). These five characteristics help organizational systems relate with each other. The evolution of systems theory has focused on how independent organizational systems can, when influenced by chaotic events, result in a reorganization of the organization, and increase the effectiveness of leadership practices. To further assist leaders with monitoring the existing environment and help identify organizational chaos, leaders may benefit from application of the degrees of freedom model.

Degrees of freedom model. Based on the themes identified from the research study, the degrees of freedom model may help credit union leaders monitor the existing environment and help identify organizational chaos. To assist credit unions with identifying organizational chaos, the degrees of freedom model has positive and negative degree variances from what leaders identify as normal operations. As changes in the internal or external operating environment occur, credit union leaders can measure the change against normal operations and develop strategies in response to the degree of chaos.

A potential practical application of the degrees of freedom model is measuring return on assets in credit unions. A common credit union measurement is return on assets (ROA). Return on assets is the percentage of net operating income before reserving for allowance for loan loss, after paying for the cost of deposits paid in the form of interest on customer deposits, and reserve transfers for non-operating gain or losses (National Credit Union Administration, 2010a). A financially sound credit union is an organization with a return on assets above 1% (National Credit Union Administration, 2010a).

Using the degrees of freedom model, credit union leaders may establish 1% return on assets as normal operations. Credit union leaders may set changes to capital in quarter-degree increments. If normal return on assets was set at 1%, one-degree negative and positive freedom could be set at 0.75%, two-degrees of negative and positive freedom could be set at 0.50%, and three-degrees of negative and positive freedom could be set at 0.25%. As external environmental changes occur, and places pressure on return on assets, the degrees of freedom model can help credit union leaders identify if the environmental changes are emerging chaos or actual chaos.

Figure 2. Degrees of Freedom Model.

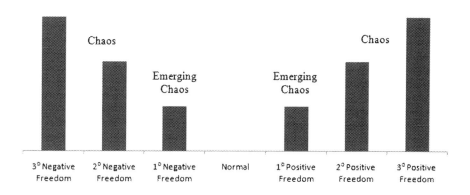

Positive or negative changes can influence an organization's ability to meet organizational strategic goals, negatively influence internal and external relationships, and place pressure on an organization's balance sheet, specifically capital and earnings. The speed at which change occurs can quickly create nonlinear dynamics within an organization. During a period of chaos, the change may occur at a faster rate than leaders and followers are able to comprehend (Guastello, 2008; Samli, 2006). Leadership skill development that may be challenged by rapid positive and negative changes to the normal operating environment can include maintaining organizational consistency (Jalonen & Lonnqvist, 2009), innovation, identifying resources, and increasing control over resources (Barber & Warn, 2005).

Based on the findings of the research study, participants indicated that they first noticed the external environmental changes that threatened the organization was the rate of financial institutions failures, rapid decrease in mortgage backed securities value, rapid stock market decline, and media reports of instability in the financial markets. As the danger signals increased, the first signs of internal dysfunction included the speed at which the regulatory environment was changing, organizational profitability, management team required to deal with more issues, increased deposits and a decrease in loan demand, and decrease in loan performance that caused an increase in loan delinquencies.

If an organization were to rapidly experience a one degree of freedom shift, either negatively or positively, then the one degree of freedom shift could represent the emergence of chaos. Organizational leaders should proceed with caution to avoid the organization emerging into actual chaos. To help leaders avoid emerging into chaos, leaders may benefit from information that is factual, empirical, survey, opinion, tracking and analyzing organizational trends, leadership's ability to anticipate change, and creating internal and external value.

If the organization were to experience two degrees of freedom, negatively or positively, the organization would emerge into chaos requiring rapid organizational response. The rapid organizational response could force leaders to re-visit the existing strategic plans or to create new strategies. The organizational operation model helps organizational leaders navigate through chaos, re-establish a new operating environment, and identify a new organizational stability environment. Once the organization has reached three degrees of freedom, either negatively or positively, instant organizational response is needed on behalf of leaders, which requires rapid problem solving and the potential for leaders not solving the right problem.

Participants described the experiences over the past two years as controlled chaos, chaotic, external chaos but not internal chaos, and the situation was not necessarily chaotic but could have become chaotic if they had not taken action. The degrees of freedom model can help leaders to better define chaotic events, to develop plans to help limit the effects of chaos on the organization, and to regain normal operations as defined by the organization. Chaos theory may help increase the understanding of the potential practical application of the organizational operational model.

As the marketplace changes, leaders should act quickly to return the organization to the zone of stability. During the period of chaos, leaders should recognize that the current state of chaos might demand a redesign, to improve product potency (Gharajedaghi, 2005). Leaders often manage in different operational zones, each of which can occur at any moment. The first zone is the zone of stability, in which the organization is sheltered from external changes (Bums, 2002). This zone is the normal operations degree in within the degrees of freedom model. The second zone is the zone of strange attractor, in which the organization remains bound to the purpose, vision, and core values of the organization (Bums, 2002). This zone is the negative one-degree or positive one degree within the degrees of freedom model. The third zone is the zone of randomness, in which chaos occurs (Bums, 2002). This zone is the negative second and third degrees or positive two or three degrees within the degrees of freedom model. Within the zone of strange attractor, organizational leaders attempt to reorganize and discover new ways to express purpose, vision, and core values with internal and external stakeholders and never settle at a fixed-point (Bums, 2002). The zone of strange attractor can cause unpredictable actions by organizational leaders and stakeholders (Potocan & Mulej, 2009).

Leadership practices that may assist leaders strengthen leader and follower relationships when transitioning through the positive or negative degrees of freedom is the situational leadership theory. In their situational leadership theory, leaders create an environment where leaders and followers choose between being tasked oriented or identifying and building relationships that increase productivity and influence organizational culture. Leaders who create an environment that focuses on task behaviors influence follower relationships by focusing on what followers should do, when followers should perform, and how followers perform (Hughes, Ginnett, & Curphy, 2002).

Recommendations for Future Research

The research may lead to a better understanding of how credit union leaders respond to organizational crises. Represented in the organizational operation model found in Figure 1 and the degrees of freedom model found in Figure 2, leaders may use these models to identify chaos, develop strategies to respond to chaos, and create a new operational norms based on chaotic experiences. The decisions made by leaders can influence various internal organizational variables and the decision-making process can have far-reaching organizational sustainability implications (McKenzie, Woolf, van Winkelen, & Morgan, 2009). The research study concentrated on the lived experiences of recognizing the signals of impending crisis, how these signals were interpreted, the relationship between such events, and leadership responses to these events. Three recommendations for future research are suggested by the research study.

The first area for future research might involve focusing on how credit union leaders respond to organizational crisis caused by negative changes in the general internal and external environment by focusing on different credit union asset sizes. As credit unions increase in size, operational complexity may also increase due to increase staff sizes, the number of products and services offered, availability of resources, and branch structures. A comparison of the signals and signs of impending chaos and leadership response to chaos by different assets size, which could include sampling credit unions under $50 million, $50 million to $100 million, $100 million to $500 million, and $500 or more, could identify the relationship between chaos complexity and chaos.

The second area for future research may include other segments of the organization instead of focusing on CEOs, CFOs, vice presidents, and senior managers of credit unions who influence strategy development for their organizations. By including other segments, researchers may recognize how followers respond to negative changes in the general internal and external environment, how chaos influences organizational operations, and potentially examine followers response to chaotic events through the leader-member exchange theory. Graen and Scandura (1987) theorized that leader and follower relationships increase through mutually agreed upon exchanges of performance standards. Followers believe in an obligation to the organization, while leaders create an environment where followers are encouraged to go beyond day-to-day performance standards, and followers are encouraged to seek experiences that are challenging (Stark & Poppler, 2009).

The third area for future research may include expanding beyond the State of Texas to include other states such as California, New York, Florida, and Nevada. By interviewing credit union leaders from other states, future researchers can continue the research study focus and investigate the lived experiences of selected top leaders and managers of credit unions faced with the crisis of a rapidly contracting economy from additional geographic locations. By incorporating other geographic locations, future researchers may identify how organizational leaders may learn to make better-informed decisions in times of uncertainty.

Summary

The purpose of the research study, using exploratory qualitative phenomenological research, was to explore the experiences, perceptions, attitudes, and behaviors of leaders in charge of individual credit unions during a period of economic contraction. The qualitative method selected was appropriate for the research study because a qualitative method is exploratory and seeks thematic rather than numerical data (Creswell, 2005). The data generated and used for the research were the participants' recollections of certain events, perceptions, interpretations, and decisions that occurred during the credit crisis and recession of 2008-2010. These elements were obtained through intensive open-ended interviews.

The contents of chapter 5 provided a final phenomenological analysis of the interview data along with a discussion of potential implications, recommendations for future action, and suggestions for future research. Recommendations for future research include focusing on how credit union leaders respond to organizational crisis by focusing on different credit union asset sizes, examining other segments of the organization instead of focusing on CEOs, CFOs, vice presidents, and senior managers, and expanding beyond the State of Texas and include other states, such as California, New York, Florida, and Nevada.

References

Aalbers, M. B. (2009). Wrong assumptions in the financial crisis. *Critical Perspectives on International Business*, *5*, 94-97. doi:10.1108/17422040910938712

Adair, J. (2003). *The inspirational leader: How to motivate, encourage, and achieve success*. Philadelphia, PA: Kogan Page US.

Ahmadi, H., Kuhle, J. A., & Varshney, S. (2010). Stress test for the financial optimization models during the 2009 recession. *Journal of Business & Economics Research*, *8*, 107.

Aldag, R. J., & Antonioni, D. (2000). *Mission values and leadership styles in credit unions*. Madison, WI: Filene Research Institute.

Allen, R. E., & Snyder, D. (2009). New thinking on the financial crisis. *Critical Perspectives on International Business*, *5*, 36-55. doi:10.1108/17422040910938677

Altman, R. C. (2009). The great crash, 2008: A geopolitical setback for the west. *Foreign Affairs*, *88*, 2-13.

Anderson, J. A. (2009). When a servant-leader comes knocking. *Leadership & Organization Development Journal*, *30*, 4-15. doi:10.1108/01437730910927070

Arciszewski, T., Sauer, T., & Schum, D. (2003). Conceptual designing: Chaos-based approach. *Journal of Intelligent & Fuzzy Systems*, *13*, 45-61.

Backstrom, T. (2009). How to organize for local resource generation. *The Learning Organization*, *16*, 223-236. doi:10.1108/09696470910949944

Baigent, G. G., & Massaro, V. G. (2005). Derivatives and the 1987 market crash. *Management Research News*, *28*, 94-105. doi:10.1108/01409170510784742

Baigent, G. G., & Massaro, V. G. (2009). Revisiting derivative securities and the 1987 market crash: Lessons for 2009. *Review of Accounting and Finance, 8,* 176. doi:10.1108/14757700910959501

Barber, E., & Warn, J. (2005). Leadership in project management: From firefighter to firelighter. *Management Decision, 43,* 1032-1039. doi:10.1108/00251740510610026

Barbour, R. S. (2001). Checklists for improving rigor in qualitative research: A case of the wagging the dog. *British Medical Journal, 322,* 1115-1117. doi:10.1136/bmj.322.7294.1115

Barron, D. N., & Hannan, M. T. (1994). A time to grow and a time to die: Growth and mortality of credit unions in New York City. *American Journal of Sociology, 100,* 381-422. doi:10.1086/230541

Basu, S., Raj, M., & Tchalian, H. (2008). A comprehensive study of behavioral finance. *Journal of Financial Service Professionals, 62,* 51-62.

Bauer, K. (2006). Detecting abnormal credit union performance. *Journal of Banking & Finance, 32,* 573-586. doi:10.1016/j.jbankfin.2007.04.022

Benbya, H., & McKelvey, B. (2006). Toward a complexity theory of information systems development. *Information Technology & People, 19,* 12-34. doi:10.1108/09593840610649952

Beugré, C. D., Acar, W., & Braun, W. (2006). Transformational leadership in organizations: An environment-induced model. *International Journal of Manpower, 27,* 52. doi:10.1108/01437720610652835

Bhal, K. T., Gulati, N., & Ansari, M. A. (2009). Leader-member exchange and subordinate outcomes: Test of a mediation model. *Leadership & Organization Development Journal, 30,* 106-125. doi:10.1108/01437730910935729

Blalock, G., Gertler, P. J., & Levine, D. I. (2008). Financial constraints on investment in an emerging market crisis. *Journal of Monetary Economics, 55,* 568-591. doi:10.1016/j.jmoneco.2008.01.005

Bloch, B. W. (1989). Chaos: Making a new science. *Southern Economic Journal, 55,* 779-780. doi:10.2307/1059589

Bloch, D. P. (2005). Complexity, chaos, and nonlinear dynamics: A new perspective on career development theory. *The Career Development Quarterly, 53,* 194.

Bloomberg, L. D., & Volpe, M. (2008). *Completing your qualitative dissertation: A roadmap from beginning to end.* Thousand Oaks: Sage Publications.

Boje, D. M. (2006). What happened on the way to postmodern. *Qualitative Research in Organizations and Management*, *1*, 22. doi:10.1108/17465640610666624

Bontis, N., & Serenko, A. (2009). A causal model of human capital antecedents and consequents in the financial services industry. *Journal of Intellectual Capital*, *10*, 53-69. doi:10.1108/14691930910922897

Bordo, M. D. (2007). The crisis of 2007: The same old story, only the players have changed. In D. D. Evanoff, D. S. Hoelscher, & G. G. Kaufman (Eds.), *Globalization and systemic risk* (pp. 39-50). Hackensack: World Scientific Publishing.

Breakwell, G. M. (2004). *Doing social psychology research*. Oxford, United Kingdom: Blackwell Publishing.

Brewer, E., & Marie, A. (2010). Be careful what you wish for: The stock market reactions to bailing out large financial institutions. *Journal of Financial Regulation and Compliance*, *18*, 56-69. doi:10.1108/13581981011019633

Bryman, A., & Bell, E. (2007). *Business research methods* (2nd ed.). New York: Oxford University Press.

Bums, J. S. (2002). Chaos theory and leadership studies: Exploring uncharted seas. *Journal of Leadership & Organizational Studies*, *9*, 42-57. doi:10.1177/107179190200900204

Burns, J. M. (1978). *Leadership*. New York: Harper & Row.

Carr-Chellman, A. A., Beabout, B., Alkandari, K. A., Almeida, L. C., Gursoy, H. T., Ma, Z., . . . Modak, R. (2008). Change in chaos: Seven lessons learned from Katrina. *Educational Horizons*, *87*, 26-39.

Cassell, C., & Symon, G. (2006). Taking qualitative methods in organization and management research seriously. *Qualitative Research in Organizations and Management*, *1*, 4-12. doi:10.1108/17465640610666606

Cassell, M. K., & Hoffmann, S. M. (2009). Not all housing GSEs are alike: An analysis of the Federal Home Loan Bank system and the foreclosure crisis. *Public Administration Review*, *69*, 613. doi:10.1111/j.1540-6210.2009.02010.x

Centini, L. (2005). *Credit union CEO leadership profile: 2000-2004*. Madison, WI: Credit Union Executives Society.

Clegg, S., Kornberger, M., & Pitsis, T. (2005). *Managing and organizations*. London: Sage Publications.

Cohen, L., Manion, L., & Morrison, K. (2007). *Research methods in education* (6th ed.). New York: Routledge.

Colbert, A., Kristof-Brown, A., & Barrick, M. (2006). *The effect of transformational leadership at credit unions*. Madison, WI: Filene Research Institute.

Cooke-Davies, T., Cicmil, S., Crawford, L., & Richardson, K. (2007). We're not in Kansas anymore, Toto: Mapping the strange landscape of complexity theory and its relationship to project management. *Project Management Journal, 38,* 50-61.

Couch, M., & McKenziem H. (2006). The logic of small samples in interview based qualitative research. *Social Science Information, 45,* 438-499. doi:10.1177/0539018406069584

Credit Union National Association. (2009a). *Cooperative activity in Canada*. Retrieved from http://www.creditunion.coop/history/canada.html

Credit Union National Association. (2009b). *Cooperative activity in Europe*. Retrieved from http://www.creditunion.coop/history/1stcoops.html

Credit Union National Association. (2009c). *Credit union activity in America*. Retrieved from http://www.creditunion.coop/history/wakeup.html

Creswell, J. W. (2005). *Educational research: Planning, conducting, and evaluating quantitative and qualitative research* (2nd ed.). Upper Saddle River, NJ: Pearson Education.

Creswell, J. W. (2009). *Research design: Qualitative, quantitative, and mixed methods approaches* (3rd ed.). Thousand Oaks, CA: Sage Publications.

Creswell, J. W., & Plano-Clark, V. L. (2007). *Designing and conducting mixed methods research*. Thousand Oaks, CA: Sage Publications.

Crossan, M., Vera, D., & Nanjad, L. (2008). Transcendent leadership: Strategic leadership in dynamic environments. *The Leadership Quarterly, 19,* 569-581. doi:10.1016/j.leaqua.2008.07.008

Crutchfield, E. B. (2000). *Developing human capital in American manufacturing: A case study of barriers to training and development*. New York: Garland Publishing.

CU Data. (2010). *Credit Unions in Texas*. Retrieved from http://credituniondirectory.net/Texas-credit-unions.html

Das, T. K., & Kumar, R. (2010). Interpartner sensemaking in strategic alliances. *Management Decision, 48*, 17-36. doi:10.1108/00251741011014436

Davidson, P., & Rowe, J. (2009). Systematising knowledge management in projects. *International Journal of Managing Projects in Business, 2*, 561-576. doi:10.1108/17538370910991142

Davies, L. (2004). *Education and conflict.* New York: Routhledge Falmer.

Defee, C. C., Esper, T., & Mollenkopf, D. (2009). Leveraging closed-loop orientation and leadership for environmental sustainability. *Supply Chain Management, 14*, 87-98. doi:10.1108/13598540910941957

Deng, L., & Gibson, P. (2009). Mapping and modeling the capacities that underlie effective cross-cultural leadership. *Cross Cultural Management, 16*, 347-366. doi:10.1108/13527600911000339

Denzin, N. K., & Lincoln, Y. S. (2005). *The Sage handbook of qualitative research* (3rd ed.). Thousand Oaks, CA: Sage Publications.

Depository Institutions Deregulation and Monetary Control Act of 1980, Pub. L. No. 96-221, § 101, 107, 117, 205, 207, 302, 304, 305, 307, and 308, 94 Stat. 132 (1980).

Dolan, S. L., & Garcia, S. (2002). Managing by values: Cultural redesign for strategic organizational change at the dawn of the twenty-first century. *Journal of Management Development, 21*, 101-117. doi:10.1108/02621710210417411

Dolan, S. L., Garcia, S., & Auerbach, A. (2003). Understanding and managing chaos in organizations. *International Journal of Management, 20*, 23-36.

Dyck, L. R., Caron, A., & Aron, D. (2006). Working on the positive emotional attractor through training in health care. *Journal of Management Development, 25*, 671-688. doi:10.1108/02621710610678481

Ellingson, L. L. (2009). *Engaging crystallization in qualitative research.* Thousand Oaks, CA: Sage Publications.

Fay, E., & Riot, P. (2007). Phenomenological approaches to work, life and responsibility. *Society and Business Review, 2*, 145-152. doi:10.1108/17465680710757367

Federal Credit Union Act, 12 U.S.C. § 1751 (1934).

Fischer, C. T. (2009). Bracketing in qualitative research: Conceptual and practical matters. *Psychotherapy Research, 19*, 583-590. doi:10.1080/10503300902798375

Fitzgerald, L. A., & van Eijnatten, F. M. (2002). Reflections: Chaos in organizational change. *Journal of Organizational Change Management, 15,* 402-412. doi:10.1108/09534810210433700

Fitzpatrick, R. L. (2007). A literature review exploring values alignment as a proactive approach to conflict management. *International Journal of Conflict Management, 18,* 280-305. doi:10.1108/10444060710826007

Flick, U. (2006). *An introduction to qualitative research* (3rd ed.). Thousand Oaks, CA: Sage Publications.

Flood, A. (2010). Understanding phenomenology. *Nurse Researcher, 17,* 7.

Foo, C. T. (2008). Conceptual lessons on financial strategy following the US sub-prime crisis. *The Journal of Risk Finance, 9,* 292-302. doi:10.1108/15265940810875612

French, S. (2009). Cogito ergo sum: exploring epistemological options for strategic management. *Journal of Management Development, 28,* 18-37. doi:10.1108/02621710910923845

Fukushige, A., & Spicer, D. P. (2007). Leadership preferences in Japan: An exploratory study. *Leadership & Organization Development Journal, 28,* 508. doi:10.1108/01437730710780967

Geraldi, J. G. (2009). Reconciling order and chaos in multi-project firms. *International Journal of Managing Projects in Business, 2,* 149-158. doi:10.1108/17538370910930572

Gerding, E. F. (2009). Code, crash, and open source: The outsourcing of financial regulation to risk models and the global financial crisis. *Washington Law Review, 84,* 127.

Gessler, N. (2007). On the order of chaos: Social anthropology and the science of chaos. *American Anthropologist, 109,* 574-576. doi:10.1525/aa.2007.109.3.574

Gharajedaghi, J. (2005). *Systems thinking: Managing chaos and complexity: A platform for designing business architecture* (2nd ed.). Boston: Butterworth-Heinemann.

Glass, C. J., & McKillop, D. G. (2006). The impact of differing operating environments on US credit union performance, 1993-2001. *Applied Financial Economics, 16,* 1285-1300. doi:10.1080/09603100500426713

Gleick, J. (1987). *Chaos: Making a new science.* New York: Penguin Books.

Goldman, E., Plack, M., Roche, C., Smith, J., & Turley, C. (2009). Learning in a chaotic environment. *Journal of Workplace Learning, 21*, 555-574. doi:10.1108/13665620910985540

Golembiewski, R. T. (2000). *Handbook of organizational consultation* (2nd ed.). New York: Marcel Dekker.

Goodhart, C. A. E. (2008). The regulatory response to the financial crisis. *Journal of Financial Stability, 4*, 351-358. doi:10.1016/j.jfs.2008.09.005

Gorton, G. (2008). The subprime panic. *European Financial Management, 15*, 10-46. doi:10.1111/j.1468-036X.2008.00473.x

Graen, G. B., & Scandura, T. A. (1987). Toward a psychology of dyadic organizing. *Research in Organizational Behavior, 9*, 175-208.

Guastello, S. J. (2008). Chaos and conflict: Recognizing patterns. *Emergence: Complexity and Organization, 10*, 1-10.

Guinnane, T. W. (2001). Cooperatives as information machines: German rural credit cooperatives, 1883-1914. *The Journal of Economic History, 61*, 366-390. doi:10.1017/S0022050701028042

Gustafson, J. (2009). Banks, credit unions cut back sharply on branch plans here. *Journal of Business, 24*, B1.

H. Res. 1151, 105d Cong., Cong. Rec. 144 (1998) (enacted).

Hall, M. J. (2008). The sub-prime crisis, the credit squeeze and Northern Rock: The lessons to be learned. *Journal of Financial Regulation and Compliance, 16*, 19-34. doi:10.1108/13581980810853190

Hames, R. D. (2007). *The five literacies of global leadership: What authentic leaders know and you need to find out*. San Francisco, CA: John Wiley & Sons.

Haro, L., & Sullivan, M. (2009). The American mortgage crisis goes global. *Critique, 37*, 51-65. doi:10.1080/03017600802598195

Healy, M., & Perry, C. (2000). Comprehensive criteria to judge validity and reliability of qualitative research within the realism paradigm. *Qualitative Market Research: An International Journal, 3*, 118-126. doi:10.1108/13522750010333861

Helbing, D. (2008). *Managing complexity: Insights, concepts, applications*. New York: Springer.

Higgs, M., & Rowland, D. (2005). All changes great and small: Exploring approaches to change and its leadership. *Journal of Change Management, 5*, 121-151. doi:10.1080/14697010500082902

Hite, J. A. (1999). *Learning in chaos: Improving human performance in today's fast-changing volatile organizations.* Houston, TX: Gulf Publishing Company.

Hock, D. (1999). *Birth of the chaordic age.* San Francisco: Berrett-Koehler Publishers.

Holland, J. H. (1995). *Hidden order: How adaptation builds complexity.* New York: Basic Books.

House, R. J. (1971). A path-goal theory of leadership effectiveness. *Administrative Science Quarterly, 16,* 321-329. doi:10.2307/2391905

Hubler, A. W., & Phelps, K. C. (2007). Guiding a self-adjusting system through chaos: Research Articles. *Complexity, 13,* 62-66.

Hughes, R. L., Ginnett, R. C., & Curphy, G. J. (2002). *Leadership: Enhancing the lessons of experience.* New York: McGraw-Hill.

Hughes, S. (2009). Leadership, management and sculpture: How arts based activities can transform learning and deepen understanding. *Reflective Practice, 10,* 77-90. doi:10.1080/14623940802652854

Jalonen, H., & Lonnqvist, A. (2009). Predictive business: Fresh initiative or old wine in a new bottle. *Management Decision, 47,* 1595-1609. doi:10.1108/00251740911004709

Johnson, L. D., & Neave, E. H. (2008). The subprime mortgage market: Familiar lessons in a new context. *Management Research News, 31,* 12-26. doi:10.1108/01409170810845921

Karp, T., & Helgo, T. T. (2009). Reality revisited leading people in chaotic change. *Journal of Management Development, 28,* 81-93. doi:10.1108/02621710910932052

Kauffman, S. (1993). *The origins of order: Self-organization and selection in evolution.* New York: Oxford University Press.

Kavanagh, M. H., & Ashkanasy, N. M. (2006). The impact of leadership and change management strategy on organizational culture and individual acceptance of change during a merger. *British Journal of Management, 17,* 81-103. doi:10.1111/j.1467-8551.2006.00480.x

Kiel, D. (1997). Embedding chaotic logic into public administration thought: Requisites for the new paradigm. *Public Administration and Management, 2.*

Kiel, L. D., & Elliott, E. (1997). *Chaos theory in the social sciences: Foundations and applications.* Ann Arbor: University of Michigan Press.

Kim, K., Payne, G. T., & Tan, J. A. (2006). An examination of cognition and affect in strategic decision-making. *International Journal of Organizational Analysis, 14*, 277-294. doi:10.1108/19348830610849709

Kramer, E. C. (2007). *Organizing doubt: Grounded theory, army units, and dealing with dynamic complexity.* Portland, OR: Copenhagen Business School Press.

Lablans, W., & Oerlemans, J. (2006). NOWCAST: Honors. *Bulletin of the American Meteorological Society, 87*, 1662-1668. doi:10.1175/BAMS-87-12-1662

Lauser, B. (2010). Post-merger integration and change processes from a complexity perspective. *Baltic Journal of Management, 5*, 6-27. doi:10.1108/17465261011016531

Lerner, V. S. (2007). Systems science, information systems theory, and informational macrodynamics: Review. *Kybernetes, 36*, 192-224. doi:10.1108/03684920710741224

Lillis, A. (2008). Qualitative management accounting research: rationale, pitfalls and potential. *Qualitative Research in Accounting & Management, 5*, 239-246. doi:10.1108/11766090810856787

Lorenz, E. (1993). *The essence of chaos.* London: UCL Press.

Lorenz, E. N. (1963). Deterministic nonperiodic flow. *Journal of the Atmospheric Sciences, 20*, 130-141. doi:10.1175/1520-0469(1963)020<0130:DNF>2.0.CO;2

Lunenburg, F. C., & Irby, B. J. (2008). *Writing a successful thesis or dissertation: Tips and strategies for students in the social and behavioral sciences.* Thousand Oaks, CA: Corwin Press.

Macintosh, G. (2007). Customer orientation, relationship quality, and relationship benefits to the firm. *Journal of Services Marketing, 21*, 150-159. doi:10.1108/08876040710746516

Magi, T. (2008). A study of US library directors' confidence and practice regarding patron confidentiality. *Library Management, 29*, 746-756. doi:10.1108/01435120810917341

Mainelli, M. (2008). Liquidity=Diversity. *The Journal of Risk Finance, 9*, 211-217. doi:10.1108/15265940810853968

Mandel, D. R. (1995). Chaos theory, sensitive dependence, and the logistic equation. *American Psychologist, 50*, 106-107. doi:10.1037//0003-066X.50.2.106

Marks, R. E. (2008). The dominoes fall: A timeline of the squeeze and crash. *Australian Journal of Management, 33,* i-xx. doi:10.1177/031289620803300201

Marques, J. F. (2007). The interconnectedness between leadership and learning: A reaffirmation. *Journal of Management Development, 26,* 918-932. doi:10.1108/02621710710833388

Marques, J. F. (2008). Awakened leadership in action: A comparison of three exceptional business leaders. *Journal of Management Development, 27,* 812-823. doi:10.1108/02621710810895640

Marshall, C., & Rossman, G. B. (2006). *Designing qualitative research* (4th ed.). Thousand Oaks, CA: Sage Publications.

Mason, R. B. (2007). The external environment's effect on management and strategy: A complexity theory approach. *Management Decision, 45,* 10-28.

Mason, R. B., & Staude, G. (2009). An exploration of marketing tactics for turbulent environments. *Industrial Management & Data Systems, 109,* 173-190. doi:10.1108/02635570910930082

Mazumder, M. I., & Ahmad, N. (2010). Greed, financial innovation, or laxity of regulation: A close look at into the 2007-2009 financial crisis and stock market volatility. *Studies in Economics and Finance, 27,* 110-134. doi:10.1108/10867371011048616

McEvoy, P., & Richards, D. (2006). A critical realist rationale for using a combination of quantitative and qualitative methods. *Journal of Research in Nursing, 11,* 66-78. doi:10.1177/1744987106060192

McKenna, R. J., & Martin-Smith, B. (2005). Decision making as a simplification process: New conceptual perspectives. *Management Decision, 43,* 821. doi:10.1108/00251740510603583

McKenzie, J., Woolf, N., Van Winkelen, C., & Morgan, C. (2009). Cognition in strategic decision making: A model of non-conventional thinking capacities for complex situations. *Management Decision, 47,* 209-232. doi:10.1108/00251740910938885

Mendenhall, M. E., Macomber, J. H., & Cutright, M. (2000). Mary Parker Follett: prophet of chaos and complexity. *Journal of Management History, 6,* 191. doi:10.1108/13552520010348353

Michela, J. L. (2007). Understanding employees' reactions to supervisors' influence behaviors. *International Journal of Organizational Analysis, 15,* 322-340. doi:10.1108/19348830710900133

Moustakas, C. (1994). *Phenomenological research methods*. Thousand Oaks, CA: Sage Publications.

Murphy, L. (2005). Transformational leadership: A cascading chain reaction. *Journal of Nursing Management*, *13*, 128-136. doi:10.1111/j.1365-2934.2005.00458.x

National Credit Union Administration. (2008a). *National Credit Union Administration: Find a credit union*. Retrieved from http://webapps.ncua.gov/cgi-bin/cudataexpanded.cgi

National Credit Union Administration. (2008b, September). *NCUA fact sheet*. Retrieved from http://www.ncua.gov/NCUA%20FACT%20SHEET%20Sept2008.doc

National Credit Union Administration. (2010a). *FOIA data files: December 2009 facts and summary*. Retrieved from http://www.ncua.gov/DataServices/FOIA/foia.aspx#top

National Credit Union Administration. (2010b). *History of credit unions*. Retrieved from http://www.ncua.gov/About/History.aspx

National Credit Union Administration. (n.d.). *NCUA frequently asked questions: Q12*. Retrieved from http://www.ncua.gov/AboutNcua/ncua_faq.html#14

Neuman, W. L. (2003). *Social research methods* (5th ed.). Upper Saddle River, NJ: Prentice Hall.

Ng, P. T. (2009). Examining the use of new science metaphors in learning organisation. *The Learning Organization*, *16*, 168-180. doi:10.1108/09696470910939224

Nikolopoulos, K., & Handrinos, M. C. (2008). The future of credit unions in the United States: Evidence from quantitative extrapolations. *Applied Financial Economics Letters*, *4*, 177-182. doi:10.1080/17446540701704349

Osborn, R. N., & Hunt, J. G. (2007). Leadership and the choice of order: Complexity and hierarchical perspectives near the edge of chaos. *The Leadership Quarterly*, *18*, 319-340. doi:10.1016/j.leaqua.2007.04.003

Osborn, R. N., & Marion, R. (2009). Contextual leadership, transformational leadership and the performance of international innovation seeking alliances. *The Leadership Quarterly*, *20*, 191-206. doi:10.1016/j.leaqua.2009.01.010

Palmer, E., & Parker, D. (2001). Understanding performance measurement systems using physical science uncertainty principles. *International Journal of Operations & Production Management, 21,* 981-999. doi:10.1108/01443570110393450

Palmer, I., & Dunford, R. (2008). Organizational change and the importance of embedded assumptions. *British Journal of Management, 19,* 20-32. doi:10.1111/j.1467-8551.2008.00568.x

Patton, M. Q. (2002). *Qualitative evaluation and research methods* (3rd ed.). Thousand Oaks, CA: Sage Publications.

Peat, F. D. (2008). *Gentle action: Bringing creative change to a turbulent world.* Grosseto, Italy: Pari Publishing.

Pees, R. C., Shoop, G. H., & Ziegenfuss, J. T. (2009). Organizational consciousness. *Journal of Health Organization and Management, 23,* 505-521. doi:10.1108/14777260910984005

Perla, R. J., & Carifio, J. (2005). The nature of scientific revolutions from the vantage point of chaos theory. *Science & Education, 14,* 263-290. doi:10.1007/s11191-004-7940-3

Pleshko, L. P. (2007). Strategic orientation, organizational structure, and the associated effects on performance. *Journal of Financial Services Marketing, 12,* 53-64. doi:10.1057/palgrave.fsm.4760061

Plowman, D. A., Solansky, S., Beck, T. E., Baker, L. K., Kulkarni, M., & Travis, D. V. (2007). The role of leadership in emergent, self-organization. *The Leadership Quarterly, 18,* 341-356. doi:10.1016/j.leaqua.2007.04.004

Potocan, V., & Mulej, M. (2009). Business cybernetics – provocation number two. *Kybernetes, 38,* 93-112. doi:10.1108/03684920910930295

Priest, H. (2002). An approach to the phenomenological analysis of data. *Nurse Researcher, 10,* 50-63.

Prigogine, I., & Stengers, I. (1984). *Order out of chaos: Man's new dialogue with nature.* New York: Bantam Books.

Pryor, R. G., & Bright, J. E. (2006). Counseling chaos: Techniques for practitioners. *Journal of Employment Counseling, 43,* 2-17.

Putnik, G. D. (2009). Complexity framework for sustainability: An analysis of five papers. *The Learning Organization, 16,* 261-270. doi:10.1108/09696470910949971

Quercia, R. G., Stegman, M. A., & Davis, W. R. (2007). The impact of predatory loan terms on subprime foreclosures: The special case of prepayment penalties and balloon payments. *Housing Policy Debate, 18*, 311-346.

Reilly, D. H. (2000). Linear or nonlinear? A metacognitive analysis of educational assumptions and reform efforts. *International Journal of Educational Management, 14*, 7-15.

Reinstaller, A., & Sanditov, B. (2005). Social structure and consumption: On the diffusion of consumer good innovation. *Journal of Evolutionary Economics, 15*, 505-531. doi:10.1007/s00191-005-0265-9

Ryder, N. (2008). Credit union legislative frameworks in the United States of America and the United Kingdom: A flexible friend or a step towards the dark side. *Journal of Consumer Policy, 31*, 147-166. doi:10.1007/s10603-007-9053-2

Ryder, N., & Chambers, C. (2009). The credit crunch: Are credit unions able to ride out the storm? *Journal of Banking Regulation, 11*, 76-86. doi:10.1057/jbr.2009.14

Salem, P. (2008). The seven communication reasons organizations do not change. *Corporate Communications, 13*, 333-348. doi:10.1108/13563280810893698

Samli, A. C. (2006). Surviving in chaotic modern markets: Strategic considerations in turbulent times. *Journal of Marketing Theory and Practice, 14*, 315-323. doi:10.2753/MTP1069-6679140405

Samoilenko, S. (2008). Fitness landscapes of complex systems: Insights and implications on managing a conflict environment of organizations. *Emergence: Complexity and Organization, 10*, 38-46. doi:10.2753/MTP1069-6679140405

Schutt, R. K. (2009). *Investigating the social world: The process and practice of research* (6th ed.). Thousand Oaks, CA: Pine Forge Press.

Schwab, D. P. (2005). *Research methods for organizational studies* (2nd ed.). Mahwah, NJ: Lawrence Erlbaum Associates.

Seale, C., Gobo, G., Gubrium, J. F., & Silverman, D. (2007). *Qualitative research practice.* Thousand Oaks, CA: Sage Publications.

Senge, P. M. (2006). *The fifth discipline: The art and practice of the learning organization* (2nd ed.). New York: Random House.

Sharma, H. P., Ghosh, D., & Sharma, D. K. (2007). Credit union portfolio management: An application of goal interval programming. *Academy of Banking Studies Journal, 6,* 39-60. doi:10.2753/MTP1069-6679140405

Shiller, R. J. (2008). *The subprime solution: How today's global financial crisis happened, and what to do about it.* Princeton: University Press.

Shore, B. (2009). Challenges in leading sustainable institutional change. *Leadership & Organization Development Journal, 30,* 16-35.

Siemsen, E., Roth, A. V., & Balasubramanian, S. (2008). How motivation, opportunity, and ability drive knowledge sharing: The constraining-factor model. *Journal of Operations Management, 26,* 426-445. doi:10.1016/j.jom.2007.09.001

Smith, S. M., & Albaum, G. S. (2005). *Fundamentals of marketing research.* Thousand Oaks, CA: Sage Publications.

Sprenkle, D. H., & Piercy, F. P. (2005). *Research methods in family therapy* (2nd ed.). New York: Guilford Press.

Stapleton, D., Hanna, J. B., & Ross, J. R. (2006). Enhancing supply chain solutions with the application of chaos theory. *Supply Chain Management, 11,* 108-114. doi:10.1108/13598540610652483

Stark, E., & Poppler, P. (2009). Leadership, performance evaluations, and all the usual suspects. *Personnel Review, 38,* 320-338. doi:10.1108/00483480910943368

Stoker, J. I. (2008). Effects of team tenure and leadership in self-managing teams. *Personnel Review, 37,* 564-582. doi:10.1108/00483480810891682

Sun, P. Y., & Scott, J. (2005). Sustaining second-order change initiation: Structured complexity and interface management. *Journal of Management Development, 24,* 879-895. doi:10.1108/0262171051062703

Svensson, G. (2009). Subject trends in The History of Marketing Thought: From simplicity towards complexity. *Journal of Historical Research in Marketing, 1,* 361-370. doi:10.1108/17557500910974668

Svensson, G., Wood, G., & Mathisen, B. R. (2008). Reflexive and critical views of leadership performance in corporate accomplishment. *Journal of Management Development, 27,* 879-899. doi:10.1108/02621710810895686

Texas Credit Union League. (2008). *Credit union history.* Retrieved from http://www.creditunionmember.org/Credit_Union_History.html

Thibault, R. E. (2007). Between survival and revolution: Another community development system is possible. *Antipode, 39*, 874-895. doi:10.1111/j.1467-8330.2007.00556.x

Tonge, J. (2008). Barriers to networking for women in a UK professional service. *Gender in Management, 23*, 484-505. doi:10.1108/17542410810908848

Tosey, P., & Mathison, J. (2010). Exploring inner landscapes through psychophenomenology: The contribution of neuro-linguistic programming to innovations in researching first person experience. *Qualitative Research in Organizations and Management: An International Journal, 5*, 63-82. doi:10.1108/17465641011042035

Ukpere, W. I. (2010). Demise of a single orthodoxy and the possibility of a cooperative economy. *International Journal of Social Economics, 37*, 239-253. doi:10.1108/03068291011018785

van Eijnatten, F. M. (2004). Some suggestions for a complexity framework to inform a learning organization. *The Learning Organization, 11*, 430-449.

van Kaam, A. (1959). Phenomenal analysis: Exemplified by a study of the experience of "really feeling understood". *Journal of Individual Psychology, 15*, 66-72.

van Kaam, A. (1966). *Existential foundations of psychology*. Pittsburgh, PA: Duquesne University Press.

Walker, W. (2007). Ethical considerations in phenomenological research. *Nurse Researcher, 14*, 36-46.

Washington, R. R., Sutton, C. D., & Feild, H. S. (2006). Individual differences in servant leadership: The roles of values and personality. *Leadership & Organization Development Journal, 27*, 700-716. doi:10.1108/01437730610709309

Watson, R., McKenna, H., Cowman, S., & Keady, J. (2008). *Nursing research: Designs and methods*. St. Louis, MO: Elsevier.

Weitzner, D., & Darroch, J. (2009). Why moral failures precede financial crises. *Perspectives on International Business, 5*, 6-13. doi:10.1108/17422040910938640

Wheatley, M. J. (2006). *Leadership and the new science* (3rd ed.). San Francisco, CA: Berrett-Koehler.

Wheelan, S. A. (2005). *The handbook of group research and practice*. Thousand Oaks, CA: Sage Publications.

White, J., & Kleiner, B. H. (2001). Effective human resource management in the credit union industry. *Management Research News, 24,* 127-132. doi:10.1108/01409170110782739

Whitty, S. J. (2010). Project management artefacts and the emotions they evoke. *International Journal of Managing Projects in Business, 3,* 22-45. doi:10.1108/17538371011014017

Willis, J. W. (2008). *Qualitative research methods in education and educational technology.* Charlotte, NC: Information Age Publishing.

Wong, L. (2009). The crisis: a return to political economy? *Critical Perspectives on International Business, 5,* 56-77. doi:10.1108/17422040910938686

Woods, M., Humphrey, C., Dowd, K., & Liu, Y. (2009). Crunch time for bank audits? Questions of practice and the scope for dialogue. *Managerial Auditing Journal, 24,* 114-134. doi:10.1108/02686900910924545

Wycisk, C., McKelvey, B., & Hulsmann, M. (2008). "Smart parts" supply networks as complex adaptive systems: analysis and implications. *International Journal of Physical Distribution & Logistics Management, 38,* 108-125. doi: 10.1108/09600030810861198

Xirasagar, S. (2008). Transformational, transactional, and laissez-faire leadership among physician executives. *Journal of Health Organization and Management, 22,* 599-613. doi:10.1108/14777260810916579

Yeomans, L. (2008). It's a general meeting, it's not for us.internal communication and organizational learning: An interpretive approach. *Corporate Communications, 13,* 271-286. doi:10.1108/13563280810893652

Yiing, L. H., & Ahmad, K. Z. (2009). The moderating effects of organizational culture on the relationships between leadership behaviour and organizational commitment and between organizational commitment and job satisfaction and performance. *Leadership & Organization Development Journal, 30,* 53-86. doi:10.1108/01437730910927106

Yolles, M. (2007). The dynamics of narrative and antenarrative and their relation to story. *Journal of Organizational Change Management, 20,* 74-94. doi:10.1108/09534810710715298

Yukl, G. (2006). *Leadership in organizations.* New York: Elsevier.

Zexian, Y. (2007). A new approach to studying complex systems. *Systems Research and Behavioral Science, 24,* 403-416. doi:10.1002/sres.843

Zhong, Y., & Low, S. P. (2009). Managing crisis response communication in construction projects – from a complexity perspective. *Disaster Prevention and Management, 18*, 270-282. doi:10.1108/09653560910965637

Printed in the United States
By Bookmasters